LISTEN UP

LISTEN UP

How to Improve Relationships, Reduce Stress, and Be More Productive by Using the Power of Listening

Larry Barker, Ph.D., and
Kittie Watson, Ph.D.

St. Martin's Press ⚹ New York

www.stmartins.com

ROSE IS ROSE © UFS
Reprinted by permission.

Book design by Michelle McMillian

ISBN 0-312-24265-4

First Edition: October 2000

10 9 8 7 6 5 4 3 2 1

To Milford "Grandpa" Barker (1916–1996).
He listened. . . .

Acknowledgments

Although it would be impossible to acknowledge individually all of our students, friends, relatives, and clients who have contributed ideas and examples for this book, there are a few to whom we'd like to give special recognition. To Marian Lizzi, for seeing potential in the project and cultivating it with care. To Alice Martell, our literary agent, for needed help with the business details of the project and giving us needed encouragement. To Ann Meehan, for taking the time to read and edit many early drafts of the manuscript. Finally, to Melissa Barker, for her thoughtful feedback and suggestions during the creative process.

Contents

Contents

Contents

Contents

"When people talk, listen completely.
Most people never listen."

—ERNEST HEMINGWAY

Foreword

Listening Is the Beginning
of Understanding

We began conducting listening research and writing as a team in the late 1970s. Since that time we have developed several widely used listening assessment instruments and have written numerous papers, articles, book chapters, and books on listening. Both of us held academic positions at major universities (Kittie at Tulane University in New Orleans and Larry at Auburn University in Alabama) while simultaneously building a management-consulting firm. We are both past presidents of the International Listening Association and have appeared on NBC's *Today Show* and ABC's *20/20* as listening experts.

As you may have already guessed, we are both passionate about the potential we all have to become better listeners. If you share our passion, this book will help you grow personally and professionally.

The principles and tips in this book originated primarily from our theory and research. They have been field tested in Fortune 500 corporations, small businesses, and nonprofit organizations across the United States. Throughout the book we use examples taken from our experience with friends, family, clients, and students. We've changed names and taken some artistic license with locations and companies in order to protect confidentiality. However, the scenarios are based on real-life situations experienced by real people.

The steps to listening improvement are fairly simple. Yet it is important to remember that just because something is simple, it is not necessarily easy. The challenge is to keep focused on the benefits of listening improvement and move forward one step at a time.

Introduction

Wisdom Is the Reward
for a Lifetime of Listening

Consider the following scenarios:

- Tom and Angela never really talk anymore. They both work long hours at demanding jobs and by the time they get home they are bushed and too tired to listen. Their marriage of five years has become a "shell." They both occasionally wonder what happened to the excitement they once felt about each other. They use tiredness as an excuse to avoid having a serious discussion about their relationship.

- Thirteen-year-old Carey shouts at Allison, her mother, a lot. Often Allison shouts back and both often end up walking away in a snit. Allison, recently divorced, feels a lot of pressure to support the two of them. Carey's started using marijuana, dressing all in black and hanging out with a group obsessed with vampires. Allison is afraid that Carey is headed for deep trouble. When Allison attempts to have serious talks with her daughter, Carey rolls her eyes or maintains a deadpan expression. Allison is at her wit's end.

• Margo goes through prospective boyfriends like water. She is attractive and comes from a good family but has one irritating habit: she can't keep her mouth shut! Margo begins most relationships by telling her life story in minute detail, starting on page one. She asks a few questions, but instead of listening to her date's answers she tends to interrupt him before he can answer. Margo doesn't understand why she seldom has second dates.

• Clark is the leader of a quality action team in a midwestern nuclear power plant. His team recently missed a key milestone related to the plant's strategic plan. During meetings the team members come unprepared, interrupt each other, have side conversations, and ignore others' comments. Clark's supervisor told him that if the team didn't perform more effectively, he would be replaced as team leader and demoted.

• Jessica heads the investment relations department for a major oil company. Her job demands that she often meet clients after hours for dinner meetings. After a long day at the office, it's hard for her to regenerate enough energy to listen effectively and attentively during dinner conversations. She has been accused of not understanding her client's problems and has lost three major investors in recent months. Her job performance appraisal was extremely low last week, and she is very concerned about her future with the company.

These scenarios reflect different personalities, life situations, and challenges. However, they all have a common source: ineffective listening.

Solving these and other serious listening problems requires commitment and hard work. The first step in listening improvement involves **awareness.**

In the early 1990s a book titled *The "T" Factor Diet* topped *The New York Times* nonfiction best-seller list. This book alerted many Americans to their eating habits. While many of us were aware that eating excess fat was dangerous to our health, few of us knew how many fat grams were in particular foods or the amount we consumed on a given day. The ideas in the book, indirectly, were responsible for food manufacturers beginning to identify the number of fat grams in packaged food. In addition, low-fat menus became more available in many restaurants across the country. McDonald's even jumped on the bandwagon and offered the "McLean DeLuxe"—a lower-fat version of their regular hamburger. The "T" Factor truly was successful in helping many Americans become more aware of the impact of their eating habits.

Listening effectiveness, discussed in this book, is arguably more important for our ultimate health and well-being than the "T" Factor. Listening, like fat in foods, is something that most of us don't stop to think about much in terms of its impact on our lives. However, listening impacts the quality of relationships, job success, and personal growth.

Research has consistently demonstrated that ineffective listening habits present the most common barriers to success in relationships and careers. Consequently, in our work with students, executives, and business professionals we hear countless heartbreaking poor listening stories. Frustration, misunderstandings, and hurt feelings are among the common themes.

This book can't solve your listening problems. No book can make a commitment or do the hard work for you. However, this book can help you develop new listening habits that will ultimately change your life. If you successfully learn and practice the principles and listening tips in the following chapters, we promise that your life will never be the same. We make this promise because in the past twenty years we have had the opportunity to watch thousands of students, couples, professionals, and executives grow happier and more successful as they became more effective listeners. The examples and testimonials in this book will help you understand how practicing some key listening principles can make a difference in your relationships and your life.

1

The Power of Listening: How Listeners Control Communication

The greatest compliment that was ever paid me was when one asked me what I thought, and attended to my answer. —HENRY DAVID THOREAU

Each of us has the power to decide how and when to listen.

> Carla and Ed were on a second honeymoon vacation in Hawaii. During dinner at an intimate waterfront restaurant on Maui, Carla began talking about the good times they had shared on their first honeymoon. As she reminisced, Carla became acutely aware that Ed hadn't heard a word she said. His thoughts had wandered back to unfinished work at his office on the mainland. Carla gave Ed a reprimand kick under the table and he "jumped" to attention.

Sound familiar? Unfortunately, this scenario with different people and different topics is played out thousands, perhaps millions, of times every day. It illustrates a simple fact that, as listeners, each of has the power to pay attention or not. If we consciously or unconsciously elect not to listen—the speaker is out of luck. While speakers can learn tips and techniques to capture attention and engage listeners, no one can make us listen unless we want to. True, speakers can threaten, encourage, plead, or entertain us to make it easier for us to listen, but in the final analysis the power for successful communication rests with the listener.

Three Common Dangerous Assumptions About Listening

At the beginning of our listening seminars we often ask participants to give us some of their assumptions about listening. We have collected a list of these assumptions. Although some have merit, based on our research and experience, many of our participants' initial assumptions are totally off base. See if you have made any of the following unfounded, and at times dangerous, assumptions concerning listening.

Dangerous Assumption #1

■ **Speakers control communication more than listeners.**
Many of us believe that "having the floor" means controlling the agenda, whether in one-on-one conversation or in large groups. This

---

As listeners, we control communication when we:

- tune in and out of conversations at will
- elect whether or not to pay attention
- add our own interpretations, whether verbalized or not
- evaluate messages as important or not
- act on or respond to information at will

---

is why we spend so much time learning to speak effectively; we think speaking is the only currency for good communication.

In Reality

■ **Listeners control the dialogue.**

Think about meetings and programs you have attended. Have you ever been a member of a hostile audience? If so, you've observed listening power firsthand. No matter how skilled, charismatic, or engaging a speaker may be, we decide whether or not to listen.

> The CEO of an eastern utility corporation ran into a buzz saw at a meeting of union employees. He began his presentation with a reference to the improved safety record at the plant, but was unaware that a fatal accident had occurred that morning while he was en route. A rookie lineman had been electrocuted when he failed to put on rubber gloves to handle a hot wire. The workers at the gathering began to yell angry remarks and eventually the CEO was led out the side door by the HR representative to protect him from more verbal abuse.

If the CEO had attempted to pull rank to get his workers to listen, the situation would only have gotten worse.

■ **Speakers cannot force others to listen.**

On the other hand, listeners who are aware of their power can take full advantage of the situation.

> Joanne, a retail manager at an upscale department store in Los Angeles, gives her clothing buyers full attention when discussing their options. She asks questions, uses head nods,

smiles, and makes eye contact to control the pace of the discussion. Her buyers don't even notice that, although she speaks very little during the planning sessions, she is in full control of the outcome.

In this case, Joanne uses her listening skills to make good use of her time by demonstrating her involvement and interest.

Dangerous Assumption #2

■ **We can listen well when we really have to.**

Many of us keep our full attention "in reserve," assuming we can use it when it's really needed. This assumption can lead to overconfidence in our ability to listen effectively. We ask participants to test this assumption in each of our seminars. They are shown a twenty-second video clip about an emergency hospital situation. We ask them, before viewing the clip, to imagine that this is a life-and-death situation where high-level listening is critical. After being asked ten simple questions about what they have seen and heard, few participants can answer more than four questions correctly.

In Reality

■ **Listening harder doesn't necessarily mean listening better.**

Frieda, a seminar participant from Oregon, told us that she used to assume that through intense concentration she could remember important messages accurately. She relayed that her assumption was debunked when she filed an incorrect financial report based on her memory of a phone conversation while away from her desk. A government auditor challenged Frieda's numbers and her company had to pay a penalty as a result. She now records all information on specially prepared note pads and asks associates to confirm her notes.

■ **Listeners overestimate how much information they remember.**

Even highly trained listeners have trouble with technical and unfamiliar information. Research on retention has found that most people remember less than 50 percent of what was said immediately after a ten-minute talk. That percentage drops to less than 10 percent after twenty-four hours.[1]

AT&T has capitalized on the fact that most of us cannot remember a string of seven numbers long enough to dial them after calling information. For an additional charge, the information operator will dial the number for us—thus eliminating possible or probable listening errors. Those of us who take full advantage of our listening power can beat these percentages.

Dangerous Assumption #3

■ **When we start talking, others start listening.**

Test this assumption by thinking back to a recent meeting you attended. Were you mentally and emotionally focused to begin listening the moment the first speaker began? Or were you still thinking about the unfinished work on your desk, travel arrangements that needed to be made, or countless other items on your to-do list?

In Reality

■ **It takes time for us to engage as listeners.**

When we begin to talk, we often forget that others may not be prepared to listen. Most of us need at least a few seconds to get on track when someone else begins to speak. It's like shifting gears to let our attention mesh comfortably with the speaker's words and ideas.

In these situations, without conscious awareness and incentive, most of us have trouble listening immediately. This is one reason that public speakers have been trained to use attention-getting introductions such as startling statements, jokes, or personal anecdotes to capture listeners' attention.

■ **Furthermore, we can train ourselves to listen immediately with incentive and practice.**

> Jeremy, a college student at Auburn, couldn't understand why he never could get an A on his calculus exams. He was a bright student and was used to getting high grades. He talked to his advisor about the problem and, after several sessions, discovered a possible reason that his grades weren't higher. In most classes that Jeremy attended, professors tended to take a few minutes to talk about personal or sports issues before getting down to the content of their lectures. Dr. Agassi, the calculus professor, didn't waste time getting to the point. He began giving formulas and theorems at the beginning of class. Jeremy and many of his classmates tended to miss most items that were discussed in the opening minutes of the lecture. He mentally missed the first 10 percent of each lecture because he was not yet focused or prepared to listen. Once Jeremy started taking notes and focusing immediately as Dr. Agassi began his lecture, Jeremy earned the A's he was striving for.

With training and effort, we can change mental gears rapidly and focus on the speaker's ideas quickly.

Listening with Power

Unlike other communication skills such as reading and writing, listening is usually viewed as an innate process that requires only the ability to hear. Research reports suggest that those of us who have had specific training have more effective listening skills.[2]

Most of us learned to listen by accident. Even though listening is the communication skill we use the most, it is a skill in which we have received little or no training.[3] Because of this fact, Ralph Nichols, Emeritus Professor of Communication at the University of Minnesota, claims that our education system is upside down. He supports a federal mandate that would require listening education in both elementary and secondary classrooms.[4] One reason for the oversight has been the assumption that if we can hear, we can also listen.

> Ruth and Allen were excited when their newborn daughter, Jennifer, first responded to their voice. The doctor assured them that the baby had normal hearing. The couple assumed that because Jennifer could hear okay she would be able to listen effectively as she grew older.

Unfortunately, the ability to hear does not guarantee the ability to listen. Our listening habits are developed early in life without specific training. Surveys of elementary school curricula suggest listening is rarely required. And, since listening skill training is neglected in most elementary, secondary and college classrooms,[5] we learn listening habits from others, particularly our parents and teachers. Some of our early listening models may have been effective. Others were not so hot. Think about the listening role models you had as a child. In hindsight, how would you rate them? Without effective listening training

7

and/or role models, our chances for listening errors or accidents increase significantly.

Giving Up Listening Power

Many of us don't perform our best in school, at work, and in relationships because we never learned to make the most of our listening effectiveness. One way to become a better listener is to identify how we typically give away our listening advantage.

Tuning Out. When was the last time you found yourself tuning out of a conversation, lecture, or meeting? Were you bored or feeling rushed? Had you disagreed with what was being said or felt confused about the message? Even when our minds are thousands of miles away, we're usually pretty savvy at faking attention. In fact, our educational system has encouraged and even reinforced our ability to look like we are listening when we're not. We've gotten so adept at faking it that only the most observant among us knows how to detect the glassy-eyed stare or blank look. Unfortunately, when we tune out as listeners, we don't know what we've missed and inadvertently give up listening power.

Becoming Self-involved. Each of us has probably missed an opportunity to make a good impression by getting self-involved. An obvious way we miss out on listening power is when we forget someone's name during an introduction. When we are more conscious about how we look, someone else we'd like to meet, or what the other person is thinking, we don't listen carefully. When we are self-involved, we give up listening power.

Christian was finally invited to attend his company's leadership team meeting. In addition to filling in for his boss, he was asked to present the findings of the marketing department's latest sales pitch. Rather than listening intently to the other staff reports, he began mentally rehearsing his own presentation. After going over what he wanted to say several times, he started thinking about his slides and then evaluated what he was wearing. Christian was so focused on himself that he failed to capture ideas to share with his boss, learn the best ways to adapt his presentation to this particular audience, or interject critical information related to the strategic plan—not to mention actually listening to what the other speakers brought to the meeting.

> "When it came to listing her special talents all that came to mind was *Victoria is a good listener.* Her seventh-grade English teacher had written that on her final report card. Was there a way to translate listening into a talent? And if so, how would she describe it? *Caitlin Somers chose me as her summer sister because I was smart but quiet. She knew I wouldn't ask a million questions and get in the way.*"
>
> —*Judy Blume,* Summer Sisters

Jumping to Conclusions. Think about how you listen when a politician or family member expresses an opinion different from your own. Do you listen to the entire message before making a judgment, or do you begin by thinking the person is misinformed, ignorant, biased, or naive? When we fail to listen to a complete message before forming a response, we lose listening power. Rushing to act, thinking of the "great comeback," or "rehearsing a response" because we disagree with what someone else is saying often causes us to miss details. We've used a kind of listening shorthand instead of getting complete and accurate information.

Jake called the Gateway technical support line to get help with a software problem. When the technician starting asking questions, Jake answered politely until she said, "It sounds like a memory problem. Have you checked your temporary files?" Jake never heard her question because as soon as the technician said a memory problem, Jake thought to himself, "I have plenty of memory—this is a new machine. I wish I had gotten someone who was more sophisticated." When she finished talking, Jake responded, "I've gotten the most memory Gateway offers—that's not the problem." Twenty minutes later, Jake learned that he hadn't cleaned his temporary files—thus compromising the memory capacity—and gained new respect for the technician.

Since Jake disagreed with what he heard initially, he stopped listening. In this case, he could have saved time and frustration if he hadn't jumped to conclusions.

The Benefits of Listening Power

There are advantages to listening purposefully. Learning to listen better helps us build closer relationships and maximize our success.

Effective Listeners Are in Demand. When we ask workshop participants to create a list of people whom they consider to be the best listeners, most have very short lists. Really listening to others is an art.[6] Those of us who listen best are often listened to the most.

Fay, a divorced office manager in Albuquerque, receives more invitations to parties and social gatherings than any two of her friends combined. Her secret? She makes a conscious effort to ask questions and demonstrate her interest

The Cost of Listening Prejudice

The late Malcolm Forbes was keenly aware of the cost of listening prejudice. He is said to have told a true story that provides a prime example of the negative impact of such prejudice. According to the story, a modestly dressed man and wife attempted to get an appointment with the president of Harvard University. The president's secretary, judging instantly that such country hicks had no business at Harvard, told them that the president was too busy to meet with them. When they insisted on waiting, she realized that she would have to let them have an appointment, or else they would stay all day.

When the couple finally were allowed to enter the president's office, the woman quickly explained that their son had attended Harvard for one year and was happy there. He was killed in an accident, and the couple wanted to erect a memorial to him on campus.

The president dismissed them immediately by indicating that if everyone were allowed to build a statue for departed Harvard alumni, the campus would look like a cemetery.

The wife explained that they wanted to donate a *building* to Harvard, not a statue. The president rolled his eyes and told the couple that they must not know how much buildings cost. He asked them if they realized that Harvard's physical plant cost over seven and a half million dollars.

As the couple left the office the wife said to the husband, in earshot of the president, "If that's all it costs to start a university, maybe we should just start our own."

Mr. and Mrs. Leland Stanford left Harvard that day and traveled to Palo Alto, California, where they built Stanford University, as a memorial to their late son.

"There is an art in listening. To be able to listen one must abandon or put aside all prejudices, pre-formulations, and daily activities. When you are in receptive state of mind, things can be easily understood; you are listening when your real attention is given to something. But unfortunately we listen through a screen of resistance."   —Jiddu Krishnamurti, *The First and Last Freedom*

during conversations. She is the kind of person who makes others feel special and important. That's the kind of person who most of us like to be around.

What we are really looking for in a relationship is someone to listen to us; someone to really understand what we're thinking, feeling, and saying. When we concentrate more on listening attentively, our relationships improve.

Effective Listening Uncovers Others' Needs and Desires. Most of us have heard the old adage: "When everything else fails read the directions." The same holds true with understanding others better: "When everything else fails—listen." In the beginning of dating relationships most of us tend to show attention to each other and really try to listen. By the time our relationships have evolved into steady dating or marriage, many of us tend to take our partners for granted. No eureka here! Yet, as marriage counselors and psychologists have discovered, long-term relationships thrive with improved listening.[7]

To a casual observer it looked like Yolande and Glenn were newlyweds. They held hands and smiled lovingly at each other while walking through Central Park. Glenn sat attentively while Yolande shopped at Macy's and Yolande returned the favor when Glenn stopped by the Orvis shop to examine some new hand-tied trout flies. But what would have been more astonishing, if the observer could have been a fly on the wall in their home, is the fact that the couple really seemed interested in listening to each other. The truth is that, exactly one year earlier, Yolande and Glenn were considering divorce. Their counselor suggested a couples listening workshop and that turned the corner on their relationship.

After thirteen years of marriage, they found that they didn't really know each other very well. They agreed to try some listening exercises focusing on understanding what the other was really feeling, not just what they were saying.

Without ESP or a crystal ball, the only way to learn how to please one's partner is better listening. We want to be with others who listen to us. As we learn to listen better, we create opportunities to improve relationships.

Effective Listening Reduces Stress. When we feel listened to and understood, our stress levels fall.[8]

During a recent church retreat, a gentleman named Henry went to the leader, Kay, and asked about our listening training conducted during the Stephen Ministry. Henry wished his church had had a program. He explained that no one had visited him after he lost his wife to cancer. When Kay expressed understanding by saying, "That must have been hard. You probably wanted a chance to talk about your wife. . . ." Henry's eyes filled with tears. The emotions he'd experienced finally began to be released.

Effective Listening Reduces Meeting Time. Along with reducing stress in relationships, effective listeners reduce meeting time. An estimated forty million meetings take place each morning in the United States. Think about the amount of time wasted because of ineffective listening. Each time information has to be repeated because one person isn't listening costs the time of all group members. In a six-person group, a five-minute review would waste thirty minutes of company time. Effective listeners reduce meeting time and the number of follow-up meetings that have to be scheduled.

Effective Listening Increases Sales. Reports examining characteristics of the most successful professionals reinforce the benefits of effective listening.[9] Numerous self-help books and various magazine and journal articles emphasize that the best salespeople are great listeners. Real estate agents, in particular, are much more successful if they really listen to their potential client's needs and don't just think about the sales commissions.

> Vanna, an experienced real estate agent, spent the morning with Jeb and Linda, a couple moving to Memphis from a small town in Iowa. Before showing the couple any houses, she asked lots of questions and took copious notes. Vanna paid particular attention to nonverbal cues such as facial expressions, head nods, grimaces, and posture changes to gain clues about Jeb and Linda. In addition to discovering their price constraints and square footage requirements, she carefully listened to their interests, hobbies, and wish lists. By the time she took the couple on tour, Vanna easily narrowed the field to four houses. By listening mindfully, she knew what features would please her clients and land a sale.

In fact, when the couple made an offer on the first house they toured, Linda commented, "You're unbelievable. You found the perfect house for us. It has more features than I ever thought we'd find in a traditional home. I get a bathroom spa, Jeb gets his three-car garage, our dogs get a fenced yard, and it is within walking distance to the best school system in the city. How did you do it?"

Sales professionals who listen at their best read between the lines and know when to ask questions, clarify expectations, and repeat what was said.[10] They've also learned the importance of observing what potential customers may be saying nonverbally.

Effective Listening Improves Business Performance. American companies have often failed to listen effectively to the needs of customers, employees, and stockholders. Yet, as trade deficits increase and profits decrease, business professionals have looked for ways to improve the quality of American products and services. Successful businesses are learning that listening to employees and customers is the fastest way to improve products, services, and performance.[11] In fact, the successful Macintosh computer was created as a direct result of listening to customers. An Apple engineer listened in on a customer conversation and developed the new Macintosh as a result of customer requests. Since listening is so important to Apple customer service, the executive staff receives listening certificates when they actually answer one or more customer calls personally.[12] As Tom Peters wrote in *Thriving on Chaos:*

Today's successful leaders will work diligently to engage others in their cause. Oddly enough, the best way, by far, to engage others is by listening—seriously listening—to them. If talking and giving orders was the . . . model of the last fifty years, listening . . . is the model of the [1990s] and beyond.[13]

American business executives now realize that when they listen to their employees and customers, they gain valuable ideas and input to improve productivity and profits.

The Power to Choose

As we learn the power of listening, we begin to look at communication events very differently. Instead of being passive spectators, we try to get the most out of each listening event. Surprisingly, at times the best choice may mean choosing not to listen.

> Jessica's cubicle was at the intersection of two aisles in her office. Her cube became the informal meeting place for all who passed by going to and from the coffee machine. Most of the time Jessica enjoyed the company, but there were times when she felt frustrated when she couldn't concentrate on her work because of lengthy conversations. When she caught herself letting her mind wander to her pressing work Jessica often felt guilty.

In one of our coaching sessions, we explained to Jessica that she had a choice as a listener. Eventually she let go of her guilt and chose to listen more selectively the next time her co-workers began to tell a story she had already heard. She exercised her power to tune them out and focus her listening energy on tasks that were of higher priority to her job and career success.

In the example above, Jessica took control of the listening situation. She identified what her choices were and began to make conscious decisions about how to listen. We, like Jessica, can learn to use the power of listening.

REFERENCES

1. R. G. Nichols (1957). Listening is a 10-part skill. *Nation's Business*, 56–58; A. Wingfield and D. L. Byrnes (1981). *The Psychology of Human Memory*. New York: Academic Press.

2. J. Brownell (1990). Perceptions of effective listeners: A management study. *Journal of Business Communication*, 27, 401–15; D. Stauffer (July 1998). Yo, listen up: A brief hearing on the most neglected communication skill. *Harvard Management Update*, 10–11.

3. D. Borisoff and M. Purdy (eds.) (1997). *Listening in Everyday Life. A Personal and Professional Approach*. 2nd Ed. Lanham, MD: University Press of America; K. W. Watson and L. L. Barker (1984). Listening behavior: Definition and measurement. In R. N. Bostrom (ed.), *Communication Yearbook Eight*, Beverly Hills: Sage, 178–197.

4. R. G. Nichols (1966). Listening instruction in the secondary school. In S. C. Duker (ed.), *Listening readings* (pp. 242–243). New York: Scarecrow Press; Rhodes, K. W. Watson and L. L. Barker, (1990). Listening assessment: Trends and influencing factors in the 1980s. *Journal of the International Listening Association*, 4, 62–82.

5. F. I. Wolff and N. C. Marsnik (March 1991). 1979 and 1990 Studies: Listening instruction trends in randomly selected colleges and universities. Presented at the International Listening Association convention, Jacksonville, FL.

6. L. L. Freeman (February 1999). Re-finishing school. *Working Woman*, 84–85.

7. R. Josselson (1992). *The Space between Us: Exploring the Dimensions of Human Relationships*. San Francisco: Jossey-Bass.

8. S. M. Simonton (1984). *The Healing Family: The Simonton Approach for Families Facing Illness*. Toronto: Bantam Books.

9. B. D. Sypher, R. N. Bostrom and J. H. Selbert (1989). Listening, communication abilities, and success at work. *Journal of Business Communication*, 26, 293–301.

10. J. Fioravante and D. I. Stein (October 1998). Seller, beware: Little missteps can crush your deal. How to stay on the right path. *Success*, 54.

11. A. R. Field (February 1990). Your service underground: What the truck driver can teach the CEO. *Success*, 38; T. O. Jones and W. E. Sasser (November–December 1995). Why satisfied customers defect. *Harvard Business Review*, 43–55; S. E. Prokesch (November–December 1995). Competing on customer service: An interview with British Airways' Sir Colin Marshall. *Harvard Business Review*, 25–38; M. Stein, T. Thompson and L. Cusella (1995). The impact of organizational structure and supervisory listening indicators on subordinate support, trust, intrinsic motivation, and performance. *International Journal of Listening*, 9, 84–105.

12. T. Peters and N. Austin (1985). *Passion for Excellence*. New York: Warner Books.

13. T. Peters (1987). *Thriving on Chaos*. New York: Harper & Row.

2

Listening with a Preference: How Each of Us Has Our Own Listening Style

What you are speaks so loudly I can't hear what
you say.   —RALPH WALDO EMERSON

In the early 1980s, we began questioning how and why clients, work-shop participants, and students listen differently. We noticed that the attention and interest of listeners changed dramatically throughout lectures, workshops, or classes. We also realized that there are inconsistencies in what engages listeners. Our curiosity culminated in our development of the first prototype of the Listener Preference Profile in 1984 and the fine-tuning and completion of the instrument in 1993.[1] Since then numerous studies have contributed to the repository of research using the Listener Preference tool.

Listening preferences are determined by how, where, when, who, and what types of information we like to receive most from others. The way we choose to receive information includes whether or not we find it easier to listen to others on the telephone or face-to-face and how we prefer messages to be organized. Some of us prefer to listen in outline form; others of us like speakers who include interesting stories and examples. Most of us also prefer particular locations for listening;

19

some of us listen best when in comfortable surroundings, and others listen best in more formal settings. Some of us are morning people, while others are better listeners in the afternoon or evening. We also have likes and dislikes about the types of information we most like to hear presented. While some find it easy to listen to technical data, others may find it too dry or boring. In addition to empirical research, our profile has been used and field-tested with thousands of participants in listening seminars and presentations around the world. In 1998, ABC's *20/20* featured the Listener Preference Profile on their segment, "Talking to a Wall."[2] In our workshops and training, we use the Listener Preference Profile to help participants:

- understand the unique advantages and disadvantages of why and how they listen;
- adapt messages more effectively with their bosses and coworkers;
- determine the best approach to use with key decision-makers or audience members when selling a product, making an in-house presentation, pitching an idea, or engaging particular age groups;
- appreciate and value differences in teams and work groups.

The Listener Preference Profile is included in this book to provide a way to learn more about your own preferences as well as the preferences of others. After you have completed the profile, we will provide a description of each preference and an example from our own experiences. The examples are not intended to represent all of the characteristics a particular listener style might represent. They are designed to get you thinking about how preference traits might be expressed in actual situations. After the example, pros and cons for each characteristic provide a balanced perspective for each preference type.

Listener Preference Profile

Instructions: Think of a specific listening role or situation that you are often in. For example, you may focus on your listening at work, as a friend, as a spouse, or as a parent. (*Note:* You can complete the instrument more than one time, with different roles and situations in mind.) As you read the series of statements below, keep the particular listening role or situation you have chosen in mind. Circle the appropriate number on your answer sheet using the key below.

Always	5
Frequently	4
Sometimes	3
Infrequently	2
Never	1

1. I focus my attention on other people's feelings when listening to them.   5 4 3 2 1

2. When listening to others, I quickly notice if they are pleased or disappointed.   5 4 3 2 1

3. I become involved when listening to the problems of others.   5 4 3 2 1

4. I try to find common areas of interest when listening to new acquaintances.   5 4 3 2 1

5. I nod my head and/or use eye contact to show interest in what others are saying.   5 4 3 2 1

6. I am frustrated when others don't present their ideas in an orderly, efficient way.   5 4 3 2 1

7. When listening to others, I focus on any inconsistencies and/or errors in what's being said.   5 4 3 2 1

8. I jump ahead and/or finish thoughts of speakers.   5 4 3 2 1

9. I am impatient with people who ramble on during conversations.   5 4 3 2 1

10. I ask questions to help speakers get to the point more quickly.   5 4 3 2 1

11. I wait until all the facts are presented before forming judgments and opinions.   5 4 3 2 1

12. I prefer to listen to technical information.   5 4 3 2 1

13. I prefer to hear facts and evidence so I can personally evaluate them.   5 4 3 2 1

14. I like the challenge of listening to complex information.   5 4 3 2 1

15. I ask questions to probe for additional information.   5 4 3 2 1

16. When hurried, I let others know that I have a limited amount of time to listen.   5 4 3 2 1

17. I begin a discussion by telling others how long I have to meet.   5 4 3 2 1

18. I interrupt others when I feel time pressure.   5 4 3 2 1

19. I look at my watch or clocks in the room when I have limited time to listen to others.   5 4 3 2 1

20. When I feel time pressure, my ability to concentrate on what others are saying suffers.   5 4 3 2 1

Scoring:

Tally the number of times you circled 4 or 5 for statements, 1–5:
People-oriented = 17

Tally the number of times you circled 4 or 5 for statements 6–10:
Action-oriented = 5

Tally the number of times you circled 4 or 5 for statements 11–15:
Content-oriented = 4

Tally the number of times you circled 4 or 5 for statements 16–20:
Time-oriented = 10

Listener Preference Interpretation

You now have four scores, one for each of the four listener preferences: People, Action, Content, and Time. (They form the acronym PACT, which is apt, since when you communicate with others you are forming a pact.) Now identify the types of listening preferences for which you have the highest scores. These scores say a lot about your preferred style of listening.

To interpret your scores, use the following guidelines:

1. Preference strength is indicated by the number of scores in each of the listening preference types.

4 and 5 responses	high preference
3 response	moderate preference
2 and 1 responses	low preference
0 response	no preference

2. High scores (4 or 5) in two or more types suggest multiple listening preferences.
3. Zero scores in all the types suggest potential listening avoidance.

Four Listening Preferences

People-Oriented Listeners

People-oriented listeners are most concerned with how listening influences their relationships with others. They listen to understand the emotional states of others and usually remain nonjudgmental in how they view others. When confronted with personal problems or crises, many of us seek out people-oriented listeners. Open to most types of people, they can get overly involved with others. In fact at times people-oriented listeners can lose their objectivity when listening and get swept up in what they are hearing.

> Ted is a social worker at a large medical complex. After fifteen years of social work experience, his co-workers describe him as the most patient, caring, open listener they know. He works hard at giving and receiving clear messages by asking questions, clarifying what has been said, and repeating what he heard back to others. Unfortunately, his supervisor is concerned about his ability to meet his caseload. For the last six months, Ted has gotten behind on his reports. When confronted with the problem, his supervisor realizes that when Ted takes too much time listening to his clients and his overinvolvement with their problems causes him to miss deadlines.

Ted's listening behaviors illustrate some extreme characteristics of a people-oriented listener. Consider the following characteristics to learn more about this preference. As you do, identify the ones you notice most often in yourself.

People-Oriented Characteristics

Strengths:
- cares and is concerned about others
- is nonjudgmental
- provides clear verbal and nonverbal feedback signals
- identifies emotional states of others
- interested in building relationships
- notices moods in others quickly

Weaknesses:
- becomes overinvolved with feelings of others
- avoids seeing faults in others
- internalizes/adopts emotional states of others
- is intrusive to others
- is overly expressive when giving feedback
- is nondiscriminating in building relationships

Action-Oriented Listeners

Action-oriented listeners concentrate intensely on the task at hand. They often prefer to listen in outline form and find it difficult to listen to speakers who are disorganized. The action-oriented listener is an appreciated member of most meetings because he or she encourages others to stay on topic and to present information in a logical, organized way. At times because they appear to be overly task-driven, action-oriented listeners come across as impatient and not very interested in building relationships with others.

Melissa is an MBA student at a highly respected university. As a working mother taking classes at night, she is interested in getting the best information in the shortest amount of time. Although she avoided taking a required finance course from one professor with a reputation of having a rambling teaching style, she finally had no choice. She left the first class feeling frustrated and bored; she hadn't learned anything new. In the next class she was determined to make the best use of her time and went in prepared with a series of specific questions that helped the professor stay on track.

Action-Oriented Characteristics

Strengths:
- gets to the heart of the matter quickly
- gives clear feedback concerning expectations
- concentrates energy on understanding task at hand
- helps others focus on what is important
- encourages others to be organized and concise
- identifies inconsistencies in messages

Weaknesses:
- tends to be impatient with rambling speakers
- jumps ahead and moves to conclusions quickly
- gets distracted easily by unorganized speakers
- asks blunt questions of others
- appears overly critical
- minimizes emotional issues and concerns

Content-Oriented Listeners

Content-oriented listeners have a tendency to carefully evaluate everything they hear. They enjoy listening to details and digging below the surface to explore all aspects of a problem. At times it may appear they are looking under a microscope to dissect information. They usually prefer to listen to experts and highly credible sources. Content-oriented listeners try to see all sides of an issue and enjoy listening to challenging or complex information. They also enjoy spontaneous discussions and creative exchanges of ideas. People with technical degrees or interests are often content-oriented listeners.

> Carol is on the fast-track with a utility company. With a graduate degree in engineering, Carol has excellent analytical skills, and others look to her for input. During her first meeting of the day, a salesperson tries to sell her division a new product. As he starts talking, Carol evaluates his credentials and speaking style. As the meeting progresses, Carol makes mental and written notes about his presentation. At least once, she interrupts his talk to ask a question about one of his services. At the end of the presentation, she summarizes what was said, expresses her reservations, points out what she considers to be the strengths, and recommends he prepare a proposal addressing her concerns.

Content-Oriented Characteristics

Strengths:
- values technical information
- tests for clarity and understanding
- encourages others to provide support for their ideas
- welcomes complex and challenging information
- looks at all sides of an issue

Weaknesses:
- is overly detail-oriented
- may intimidate others by asking pointed questions

- minimizes the value of nontechnical information
- devalues information from unknown individuals
- takes a long time to make decisions

Time-Oriented Listeners

Time-oriented listeners are clock-watchers and encourage others to be the same. They value time and often get impatient with those who waste it. While they encourage efficiency and time management, their self-imposed time constraints can limit creativity. Time-oriented listeners must be careful not to interrupt or discount relationships with others.

Many time-oriented listener behaviors are easily identified with those who work in business and industry. Bob, for example, is a partner with an international law firm. It is not unusual to see him referring to his calendar or looking at one of his clocks when talking with members of his staff. About mid-afternoon, his managing partner sticks his head in Bob's office and asks, "Do you have a minute?" Bob responds, "Sure, I have about ten minutes, but then I've got to finish that client status report you wanted." Before starting the meeting, Bob closes his door, asks his secretary to hold all calls for the next ten minutes, moves what he had been working on to the side of his desk, and gives his boss his undivided attention. While Bob is conscious of time, he is also able to focus on important issues. The time-oriented listening traits that Bob uses in this business setting are usually valued. These same traits, however, may be considered troublesome at home or with friends.

Time-Oriented Characteristics

Strengths: • manages and saves time effectively
            • lets others know listening time requirements

- sets time guidelines for meetings and conversations
- discourages wordy speakers from wasting time
- gives cues to others when time is being wasted

Weaknesses:
- tends to be impatient with time wasters
- interrupts others, putting a strain on relationships
- lets time affect the ability to concentrate
- rushes speakers by frequently looking at watches/clocks
- limits creativity in others by imposing time pressure

Multiple Preferences

It isn't unusual for a person to have high scores in two or more preference categories. In fact, 40 percent of all respondents indicate at least two strong preferences.[4] In some cases the preferences complement each other, while in others they contradict one another. For example, if you were to have strong people- and time-oriented preferences, you might be more open to conversation in some settings and appear rushed in others.

Alice, a bartender, is alternately a people-oriented and time-oriented listener. Of the four bartenders who work the evening shift, she has the most regulars. One reason for her popularity is the interest and involvement that she shows her customers, especially early in the evening. When the lounge isn't busy, she listens intently to her customers' stories, problems, and heartbreaks. Alice, like most people-oriented listeners, is often more interested in stories than in the details of taking orders. As the bar gets busier, she frequently begins to feel time pressure, and Alice's people-oriented preference gradually is replaced with her time-oriented one. When she becomes time-oriented, her willingness to listen to casual conversation decreases. She begins to ask more direct questions concerning the orders and to demonstrate through her face and eyes that she is getting a bit impatient. She occasionally confuses her regular customers who have seen her only at times when the lounge wasn't busy.

When multiple preferences exist, several factors can determine which preference will come out at a given time. Some of the primary factors include:

- time pressure
- interest or motivation in speaker/topic
- communication setting
- presence of (significant) others during communication
- listening energy supply

Although multiple listener preferences are usually independent from one another, preferences occasionally overlap. One of the most common combinations involves action- and time-oriented preferences.

Ellen, an action-oriented listener, prefers to listen to highly organized committee reports. When committee members present information without a clear purpose or structural format, her time-oriented preference is also called out and she begins asking questions to get members on task, letting them know her time constraints, or she begins looking at her watch.

Multiple preferences on the Listener Preference Profile are actually multiple habits, depending on the communication situation. By knowing and understanding the situations more likely to call out a particular preference, we can begin to make conscious decisions whether to listen by habit or by active listening.

When Do Listener Preferences Emerge:

The following guidelines suggest when one preference may overshadow another:

People-Oriented. People-oriented listener preferences are dominant if:
- a relationship with the speaker is highly desirable;
- the setting for listening is informal or intimate.

Action-Oriented. Action-oriented listener preferences are dominant if:
- the listener has a low supply of energy to listen;
- the setting is more formal than informal.

Content-Oriented. Content-oriented listener preferences are dominant if:
- the listener is highly interested in the topic or speaker;
- the setting for the communication is professional or in a business contest.

Time-Oriented. Time-oriented listener preferences are dominant if:
- there is time pressure;
- the task is more important than the relationship with the listener.

No Listening Preference

About 20 percent of us indicate little or no listening preference on the Listener Preference Profile. If you scored zero in all of the categories, you may prefer *not* to gain information through listening, in certain environments and contexts. The lack of any listening preference is termed "listening avoidance." This is not necessarily a negative trait but can cause problems in extreme cases. Two of the most common causes of listening avoidance are introversion and burnout.

Listening Introversion

Introversion is a personality trait that often affects listening preference. Introverts usually prefer solitude or quiet interactions over crowds and noisy environments. Traditionally those people who are characterized as introverts prefer to work with computers, machines, and use more written communication than the average person.

> Carlos, a computer programmer, has not been promoted in ten years. A diligent worker, he is more comfortable with electronic devices than people. As a function of his introverted personality, he prefers sitting in front of a computer screen or reading a book rather than conversing with others. His colleagues find him reclusive. When communicating, he uses electronic mail, faxes, or written documents and requests that others do the same. Carlos's reluctance to communicate face-to-face or even talk on the phone has hindered his professional mobility.

If you scored zero on all of the preference types and consider yourself an introvert, this could be the main reason. Many of us, however, may enjoy the company of others and lively verbal conversations yet score low on all preference types. Listening burnout may be the culprit in this case.

Listening Burnout

If you are physically and mentally exhausted, you may have no energy left to listen. In Chapter 5, we'll discuss the concept of listening energy and burnout in greater detail. But for now, think about the frequency and intensity of talking you have been exposed to lately and determine if you feel a bit burned out as a listener. If you do, your listening avoidance is probably temporary rather than a constant preference.

> Mary Ellen, a new elementary teacher just out of college, had a strong people-oriented listening preference when she graduated. (In fact, most new teachers score very high as people-oriented listeners.) She loved children and couldn't wait to get started in her new job as a second grade teacher in Dayton, Ohio. After three months of intense teaching she returned to her parents' home at Christmas. Mary Ellen found a copy of the Listener Preference Profile in her Educational Psychology notebook and decided to take it again, just for fun. She was surprised to learn that she now had no strong listening preference. What happened?

Mary Ellen's experience is very common. Fortunately after vacations and summer breaks, most teachers tend to regain energy to listen and become more people-oriented once again. Some of our recent research with medical students also indicates a lessening of people-oriented preferences between the first and second year of medical school.[6] Bedside manners also tend to deteriorate as doctors experience burnout (not just listening burnout either.)

If your scores on the Listener Preference Profile indicate that you prefer to avoid listening, this avoidance may affect your work and relationships. It's important to remember that even though you may prefer not to listen in certain settings, you have the capacity to do so with awareness and effort. Also keep in mind that even though you may not avoid listening, other people often do. Listening avoidance, whether related to introversion or burnout, can represent a major challenge to us as speakers. Chapter 3 will explore ways to adapt to different listening preferences as a speaker.

Listener Preferences: A Few Reminders

Our listening preferences have been developed and reinforced through years of practice and develop differently in each of us. We have preferences in how and when we listen and find it easier to listen to some people than we do to others. Some of us prefer to hear only from experts, others want to be entertained, and some focus on the other person's needs. Most of us don't think about changing the way we listen, yet listening would be more efficient and enjoyable if we did. Wouldn't it be more appropriate to modify our listening when serving as jurors, attending piano recitals, chatting with friends, or participating in training seminars?

Listening Preferences Can Change

Unlike personality types and learning styles, which tend to remain constant over time, listening preferences can change rather quickly. We'll discuss some reasons why preferences may change next in this chapter. Because preferences are changeable states, and not stable traits, it's important not to label our friends and acquaintances according to one or two of their listening preferences (e.g., Sheila's a *people-oriented listener,* while Mark is a *content-oriented listener*). Labels and stereotypes can be misleading because listening preferences may change as a result of time of day, energy available, context, environment, topic, or a myriad of other factors. By learning about your preferences you will not only identify your own primary preference(s), but you will be more aware of when and why they change.

■ There is no one best way to listen.

It's important that we avoid viewing listener preferences in ourselves or others as good or bad. Each preference has characteristics that can be both positive and negative when taken to extremes. The key is to be able to adapt our listening behavior to speakers' preferences so we are on the same page as the speaker. The same principle, in reverse, holds when we are in the role of speaker. By adapting our messages to listeners' preferences, we hold their attention, get faster agreement and buy in, and often build closer relationships. In Chapter 3 we will discuss ways we can adapt to listeners with different preferences from our own.

■ Listener behaviors are influenced by time pressures and relationships.

How much time we have to listen as well as the type of relationship we have with a person influence the way we choose to listen to others. For example, because of time pressures during tax season, CPAs may interrupt co-workers who don't get to the point immediately and use strategies to abbreviate phone conversations with clients. At other less stressful times of the year, the same CPAs may display more relaxed listening behaviors, such as having leisurely conversations, giving others their undivided attention, or calling clients to just touch base. Even when we're under pressure, we usually listen differently to people we value or who have influence over us. For example, even when managers ask their secretaries to hold their calls, if their company president calls, most managers make time to listen.

■ **Understanding your listening preferences gives you a choice.**

Since preferences are habits, they do not represent your only option for listening. You do have a choice about which preference takes over. Think about it for a moment. It's unrealistic, for example, to expect conversations at a cocktail party to follow logical progressions or be structured in outline form. To impose your preferred listening style or habits on this situation would be frustrating to you and your guests. Similarly, an explanation of a complex technical problem isn't likely to be completed in sixty seconds, so a time-oriented listener would be well advised to be patient.

■ **It is difficult to switch off listening behaviors reinforced at work.**

Many executives find it difficult, if not impossible, to switch listening channels. Because certain types of listening behaviors are reinforced for at least eight hours a day, when professionals arrive home, they often forget what channel they have been using. Instead of switching to a more concerned, caring, emotional channel, many continue to use the channel they have been using at work and apply it to their spouses, children, and friends. Comments appropriate for work often come across as critical, evaluative, and judgmental of those at home. When listeners are reminded to switch channels, they can determine whether or not they are treating the people they love like employees.

Now that you understand your personal listening preferences and factors that call out both your positive and negative traits, you can work to keep your positive traits in the forefront. By understanding when and what factors are likely to call out your preference(s), you will be in a better position to regulate how you listen.

REFERENCES

1. K. W. Watson (1984). Listener Preference Profile. New Orleans: SPECTRA Communication Associates; K. W. Watson, and L. L. Barker (1988). Listener Preference Profile. New Orleans: SPECTRA, Inc.; K. W. Watson, L. L. Barker, and J. B. Weaver (1992). Development and validation of the listener preference profile. Paper presented at the International Listening Association, Seattle, WA.
2. Up Against a Wall. (January 1998). ABC *20/20*.
3. K. W. Watson and L. L. Barker (1994). Listener Preference Profile. New Orleans: SPECTRA, Inc.
4. K. W. Watson, L. L. Barker, and J. B. Weaver (1995). The listening styles profile (LSP-16): Development and validation of an instrument to assess four listening styles. *International Journal of Listening*, 9, 1–13.
5. Op. Cit.
6. K. W. Watson, C. J. Lazarus, and T. Thomas (1999). First Year Medical Students' Listener Preferences: A Longitudinal Study. *Journal of International Listening Association*, 13, 1–11.

3

Switching Channels Without a Remote: How to Adapt to Others' Listening Preferences to Improve Communication

Skillful listening is the best remedy for loneliness, loquaciousness and laryngitis.
—WILLIAM ARTHUR WARD

Sir Arthur Conan Doyle's famous character Sherlock Holmes was arguably one of the most skilled people observers of all time. He used all of his observation powers to make incredible, interesting and useful deductions.

> Sherlock Holmes . . . shook his head with a smile as he noticed my questioning glances. "Beyond the obvious facts that he has at sometime done manual labour, that he takes snuff, that he is a Freemason, that he has been in China, and that he has done a considerable amount of writing lately, I can deduce nothing else."
>
> ". . . How, in the name of good fortune, did you know all

that, Mr. Holmes?" he asked. "How did you, for example, know that I did manual labour? . . ."

". . . Your hands, my dear sir. Your right hand is quite a size larger than your left. You have worked with it, and the muscles are more developed."

". . . Well, the snuff, then, and the Freemasonry?"

". . . You use an arc and compass breastpin."

". . . Ah, of course, I forgot that. But the writing?"

"What else can be indicated by that right cuff so very shiney for five inches, and the left one with the smooth patch near the elbow where you rest it upon the desk."

"Well, but China?"

"The fish which you have tattooed immediately above your right wrist could only have been done in China . . . when, in addition, I see a Chinese coin hanging from your watch-dash chain, the matter becomes even more simple."[1]

While Sherlock Holmes is a fictitious character, his observation skills are not beyond the scope of most of us real people with lots of training and practice. Observations can also help us determine with a high degree of accuracy another person's listening preference. In the previous chapter you learned about your own listening preferences. Now we are going to focus on identifying and adapting to the preferences of others.

Knowing the preferences of others is helpful in both our speaker and listener roles. As listeners, we tend to interpret messages through the filters of our own preferences. Similarly, as speakers we tend to talk in ways that mirror how we prefer to listen. Being aware of our own preferences is the first step in improving communication. Being aware of others' preferences and adapting to them is the second and perhaps most important step.

Three Listener Preference Principles

Let's begin by focusing on some general principles that govern how our preferences impact us and others.

1. **In times of stress, most people revert to their strongest listening preference.** Since our listening behaviors are habits, under stress we usually fall back into familiar and comfortable behaviors.

> Albert was a project manager for a struggling ad agency. Usually an action-oriented listener, he was working on developing his people-oriented listener preference traits. He made a promise to himself to use more of the people-oriented traits in an upcoming meeting of the Baltimore Ad Club. At the beginning of the meeting, he tried to be more relational by asking personal questions, showing interest in other people's ideas, and observing nonverbal cues. Toward the middle of the meeting, Sarah, a sales representative for a competing ad agency, mentioned her success in getting two new clients, one of whom was Albert's.
>
> Hearing this information was a real shock. The stress Albert felt caused him to forget his plan to be more relational. Immediately his body orientation and way of relating with the group went back to his action-oriented preference. He even started interrupting others and ignored group member contributions and nonverbal cues.

Sound familiar? Albert, like many of us, is able to adapt to others much of the time when he commits to doing so. However, stress can make us forget our goals and revert to old habits.

2. **When there is little listening energy to give, we listen in ways that require the least from us.** Think back and try to remember how difficult it is to listen when you feel tired, sick, rushed, or hungry. In most of these instances, your energy reserves are used to keep your body functioning rather than to listen.

> Herb, a computer programmer, scored high in both people and content preferences. When he came down with the flu, he still felt compelled to finish a program that was critical to complete a new production system. When Mittie, his assistant, called to ask questions, Herb responded flatly. He brusquely asked Mittie to get to the point and was impatient with questions he normally would have had no trouble answering. Herb had reverted to an action preference due to the limited amount of energy he could muster to talk and listen.

Most of us prefer to avoid difficult or challenging listening situations that require concentration when we don't feel well or are dead tired. Recognizing this tendency in ourselves and others can help improve our listening effectiveness.

3. **Adapting takes practice.** Our listening preference habits are deeply entrenched. Most of the time our listening preferences work well for us. They are habits and skills we find easiest to use, and are usually best at. However, there are times when our preferences don't allow us to communicate most effectively. For example, if we have a strong *people-oriented* listening preference, it takes special energy and concentration to interact with our boss who is in a fast-paced *action-oriented* mode. Or, if we are *time-oriented* and find ourselves in a conversation with a *content-oriented* listener who wants to dig deeply into details, we can become impatient and frustrated. Even if we are aware that we

should alter listening habits to better adapt to others, it takes considerable practice.

Keep in mind that listening preferences go hand in hand with speaking preferences. As speakers we tend to give information to others in ways we prefer to receive it ourselves. Consequently, when thinking about our own listening preferences, we also need to remember to adapt to others' preferences when we are in speaking roles.

Lora was a college sophomore working nights in a coffeehouse. She had learned about listening preferences in her Communication 101 course, and had agreed to keep a log of her success in guessing and adapting to preferences of her customers for extra credit in the course. She was surprised that it took almost three weeks of practice before she remembered to adapt to her customers' preferences consistently. At first she forgot her goal after the evening rush at the coffeehouse began. Later she remembered more often to use her skill at adapting. Like many habits, it took her about twenty-one days to form the new one of evaluating and adapting to listening preferences.

As a footnote, Lora told her communication professor at the end of her sophomore year that she had been able to continue using her skill at evaluating and adapting to preferences of others on a regular basis after she completed the extra-credit project. She added that her new skills had helped her make a lot of new friends and enhance those friendships she already had.

Our advice is to begin working on adapting your listening habits to others' preferences immediately. There's no time like the present! Just accept the fact that there may be slips and falls along the way. New habits take a long time to form, but you can expect to see results in around three weeks' time.

What We've Discovered
About Listener Preferences

We have been observing and assessing listener preferences for almost twenty years.[2] When we've used the Listener Preference Profile in our classes and workshops, we have recorded the responses. Our experience suggests that undergraduate students generally have stronger people-oriented preferences and that these preferences often change dramatically once students identify a major and begin their careers. In fact, a recent longitudinal study found that first-year medical school students' preferences changed from strong people-orientation to no strong preferences by the end of their first year.[3]

We've also discovered that professional training and expertise influences a person's likelihood to demonstrate a particular listening preference. In our workshops, service professionals have a stronger inclination toward people-oriented preferences, scientists for content-oriented preferences, attorneys/financial analysts for action- and/or content-oriented preferences, teachers for people-oriented preferences, engineers for content-oriented preferences, and information/technical professionals for content-oriented preferences or no preference.

As we noted in Chapter 2, while approximately 40 percent of the general population has two or more strong preferences, another 40 percent have a single listener preference. Of this percentage, people- and action-oriented preferences are the most prevalent. About 25 percent of the general population has two listening preferences, and about 15 percent has three or four preferences.[4]

Research reports suggest that the people-oriented listener prefer-

ence is predominantly female, while content- and action-oriented listener preferences are more likely to be male traits. In examining multiple preferences, more females have the people/content combination,
while more males have the action/content combination. More males
than females also reported no particular listening preference.[5] These
results are based on research reports using American participants.
Studies conducted in other countries suggest that cultural differences
impact listener preferences.[6]

Assessing Listener Preferences

■ **Friends, Co-workers, and Loved Ones.**

The more time we spend with others, the better we are at making
educated guesses about their listening preferences. Yet we also begin to
make assumptions and often take successful communication for granted.
We may assume we know what listener preferences others have when
actually we don't. Ask yourself the following questions.

1. If you want your best friend to remember what you've said, how
   do you package your information?
2. If you want your spouse or a loved one to buy into your ideas,
   how do you present the ideas?
3. What office characteristics give you cues about whether or not
   your co-workers are people-, action-, content-, or time-oriented
   listeners?
4. What personal characteristics of your friends do you use to determine their listener preferences?

If you don't know the answers to these questions, the list of common
cues and clues for people-, action-, content-, and time-oriented listeners provided later in this chapter can help.

■ **New Acquaintances and Strangers.**

People whom we don't know very well are the most difficult to assess accurately. Initial meetings with potential employers, clients, and even dates provide special challenges as well as opportunities for us to adapt to their listener preference. By observing the environment, office, and personal cues, we can determine the best ways to communicate with each new person we meet. Keep in mind that because of the stress associated with meeting new people, our own listening habits are much more likely to interfere during first encounters.

> Fritz was somewhat nervous about meeting Jerold, the purchasing manager for a major department store chain. He wanted more than anything to make a good first impression. When he met Jerold at the China Star for lunch, he just couldn't stop talking. In fact, Fritz was so busy trying to impress Jerold that he didn't notice several cues that indicated that Jerold was on a tight time schedule. He didn't get the account, and only later (when he relayed this story in one of our seminars) did he understand that his failing to identify and adapt to Jerold's time preference cost him new business.

In this example, had Fritz noticed Jerold's frequent glances at the restaurant wall clock, or observed his early attempts at leave-taking behavior (including putting his napkin on the table, moving his chair back, and looking for the waiter), he could have easily recognized Jerold's time-oriented preference. Had Fritz done so, he could have stopped talking and ended the meeting in a timely fashion. Making quick guesses about the listener preferences of new acquaintances and successfully adapting to them can build relationships and create new business.

Listener Preference Cues and Clues

Below are lists of cues that can help provide clues to make better educated guesses about another's primary listening preferences. Remember that all cues may not be useful. In fact, some cues from office environments may even be misleading. Before guessing people's listening preference using cues from their office, determine whether or not they arranged the office decor themselves or if others did it; a person's office may actually say more about someone else or the firm rather than the person you are trying to assess. Use cues to help make a better guess than you might make by chance alone. If you make an initial assessment that is incorrect about another's preference, use feedback to modify your assessment for later conversations.

By assessing other people's preferences on a regular basis, your accuracy will improve. To begin your practice, identify one person for whom you would like to determine a listener preference. Using the cues described below, determine whether or not you would consider this person primarily to be people-, action-, content-, or time-oriented. After determining the person's preference, you can use the information to help interact with this individual more effectively.

Packaging Communication
to Match Others' Preferences

■ **Adapting to Listener Preferences When Speaking.**

After making your best guess about the preferences of another person, you are ready to begin using the information to your best advantage. Before beginning to speak, determine a strategy for the best way to communicate with your listeners. Some people may not prefer to listen and you may have to think of ways to keep them entertained or in-

	Office/Environment Cues	Personal Cues
People-oriented:	Personal pictures on walls	Makes/holds eye contact
	Personal objects in room or on desk	Varies vocal inflection
	Some clutter on desk	Smiles and nods in approval frequently
Action-oriented:	Desk organizers	Brisk, firm handshake
	Certificates and work-related pictures on walls	Speaks at a more rapid rate
	Organized bookshelves	Shows cues of disinterest such as doodling, finger taps, and foot swings
	Clean desk	
Content-oriented:	Neat stacks on desk	Serious facial expression
	Research and reference books near desk	Challenging or combative vocal tones
	Computer turned on at all times	Looks up frequently while processing information
Time-oriented:	One or more clocks observable from behind desk	Looks at watch frequently
	Has secretary call and remind him/her about appointments	Displays impatient facial expressions
	Sets reminder beeps on computer or watch	Uses beepers and other signals to indicate time

volved. Others may need a highly structured presentation. Consider using the following strategies in your next meeting.

People-Oriented Strategies:

- Tell stories and show illustrations that contain human interest value
- Use "we" rather than "I" in conversation
- Use first names
- Use self-effacing humor or illustrations

Action-Oriented Strategies

- Keep main points to three or less
- Make presentation short and to the point
- Speak at a rapid but controlled rate

Content-Oriented Strategies:

- Provide hard data when available
- Quote credible experts
- Use charts and graphs

Time-Oriented Strategies:

- Try to go under time limits when possible
- Be ready to cut out unnecessary examples and information
- Be sensitive to nonverbal cues indicating impatience or desire to leave

Remember, making faulty or incorrect assessments is not uncommon. A person may have multiple preferences or may demonstrate some cues that are confusing or contradictory. Continue to look for feedback when adapting to others to see if your strategy is working. If it isn't, be prepared to adjust on the spot.

■ Tips for Adapting to Multiple Listener Preferences

Previously we explained how preferences can complement or contradict one another. When multiple preferences exist, several factors—such as time pressure, setting, and who is present—determine which preferences are called out. Remember, multiple preferences are actually multiple habits that take over, depending on the situation. By knowing and understanding the situations more likely to call out a particular preference, you can begin to make a conscious choice about how to adapt to others.

■ Adapting to Groups.

Identifying listener preferences can help your interactions one-to-one, but interacting with more than one person creates unique challenges. Small groups and large audiences are composed of individuals with diverse experiences, education levels, genders, races, and listener preferences. When finding yourself in a staff meeting, family gathering, or public lecture, use your knowledge of listener preferences to help you handle these events more successfully.

First, keep in mind that when three or more people gather together they are likely to have multiple and/or different listener preferences. Second, you might assume your goal should be to keep everyone listening to you all the time. While ideal, it is unrealistic for you to expect to keep all listeners engaged throughout a talk or presentation.

The following are suggestions for speakers who want to adapt to the needs of different listeners.

1. **Get a feel for your target audience.** If possible, think about the makeup of your listeners in advance. Your goal is to decide how

you can best help your listeners stay tuned to what you have to say. Ask the following questions:

- Who will attend?
- Did these people come voluntarily?
- Why are they here and what do they hope to gain?
- Based on their occupations and/or interests, which preferences are these individuals most likely to have?
- Which speaker strategies should work best with the group (look at the list on page 49)?

When you can't answer these questions in advance, you may have to make an audience assessment on the spot. Consider getting to the meeting or speaking engagement early. Mingle with the crowd and get an impression about what will work best. Feel free to ask questions at the beginning of your talk. Based on the reactions, you can determine whether to use a more people-, action-, content-, or time-oriented delivery style.

2. **Use the smorgasbord approach.** Many of us enjoy smorgasbords because there is something for everyone. No matter your tastes or preferences, you'll find something you can eat. Similarly, when speaking to mixed groups, a good strategy is to provide a little taste for each preference type.

   While preparing a proposal presentation, AJ analyzes her audience quite carefully. She knows that a task force of seven people will attend. The president and primary decision-maker, Niles, is a content- and time-oriented listener. Two vice presidents and voting members, Carmen and Ralph, are almost exclusively action-oriented listeners.

Gina, a people-oriented listener, is Niles's executive secretary and influences his decisions frequently. The other two members often avoid listening situations but are required to attend and vote. Delivering a generic presentation would be detrimental to AJ's cause. In this case, she decides to focus on Niles and the secretary as her primary targets in the audience. She has thirty minutes, but plans to give a ten-minute presentation complete with handouts and visual aids. For Niles, she organizes her thoughts carefully, quotes credible sources, and supports each point with factual, concrete information. In consideration of Gina, she uses the names of task force members, personal examples familiar to Gina and nonverbally gives her special attention by smiling and looking in her direction frequently. She works to keep an energetic delivery style and asks for involvement whenever possible.

3. **Target content to the primary stakeholders.** While AJ used techniques to keep all task force members involved and alert, she was most concerned with Niles and Gina. Even though we should strive to keep all audience members as involved as possible, we must keep our targets in mind. Since you can't please everyone, decide who your real target listeners are and focus on these individuals.

4. **Keep your ideas concise.** With any listener preference, keeping ideas succinct and to the point is crucial. Even though people and content listeners are usually more accepting of longer presentations, the best suggestion is to remember to stop talking before the audience stops listening. Incorporating these guidelines should help keep your listeners with you until you finish talking.

Appreciating Differences

While it might be easier if all listeners were alike, without differences our interactions would probably be very boring. Since we don't function as clones, identifying listener preferences correctly may be difficult at first. Assessing preferences takes concentration and effort, but mastering these skills can give you a competitive advantage. In the beginning, when attempting to identify and adapt to other people's listening preferences, you may make some mistakes. At first you may forget how to apply what you have learned. You may identify the wrong preference or ignore the presence of multiple preferences. But if you are persistent, you will discover the value of understanding your own and other's preferences.

> Clashing conversational styles can wreak havoc at the conference table as well as the breakfast table. . . .
> —Deborah Tannen, *Talking from 9 to 5*

REFERENCES

1. A. C. Doyle (1976). "The Red-headed League," in *The Illustrated Sherlock Holmes Treasury*. New York: Crown Publishers, Inc., p. 17.
2. J. B. Weaver, III, and M. D. Kirtley (1995). Listening styles and empathy. *The Southern Communication Journal*, 60, 131–140; J. B. Weaver, III, K. W. Watson, and L. L. Barker (1996). Individual differences in listening styles: Do you hear what I hear? *Personality and Individual Differences Journal*, 19, 1–7.

3. K. W. Watson, C. J. Lazarus, and T. Thomas (1999). First Year Medical Students' Listener Preferences: A Longitudinal Study. *Journal of International Listening Association*.

4. K. W. Watson, L. L. Barker, and J. B. Weaver, III (1995). The listening styles profile (LSP-16): Development and validation of an instrument to assess four listening styles. *International Journal of Listening, 9*, 1–13.

5. Op. Cit.

6. C. Kiewitz, J. B. Weaver, III, H. B. Brosius and G. Weimann (1997). Cultural differences in listening style preferences: A comparison of young adults in Germany, Israel, and the United States. *International Journal of Public Opinion Research, 9*, 233–247.

4

Listening Barriers: Exploring and Overcoming Obstacles

Easy listening exists only on the radio.
—DAVID BARKAN

At the beginning of our listening workshops, we often put the words, "Listeners, Lemmings, and Black Widow Spiders" on a flipchart and ask our participants what they have in common. Most look at us with puzzled expressions and shake their heads in confusion. We then relate the following:

SCENE 1: It's almost dusk and the sky is glowing with purple hues. The setting sun silhouettes weathered, white cliffs overlooking jagged rocks spilling into the sea. In the distance, moving awkwardly and deliberately forward, is a group of small rodentlike creatures. They follow the leader, almost as if they are playing the children's game of the same name. The creatures, steadfast in their march, approach the cliff and vault over the edge into the sea, one after another. The dull thud of their bodies meeting the rocks below interrupts the silence of the evening. These creatures are lemmings.

SCENE 2: As the moon rises, two black spiders with red hourglass markings on their bellies appear to be dancing near a web that hangs in a dark corner of an old barn. The dance increases in intensity, and at the height of ecstasy the two insects become one. But the beauty of this magnificent dance is shattered as the female turns and brutally attacks the male, leaving him lifeless. The black widow spider has completed her mating ritual.

These two scenes describe two of nature's strangest paradoxes. The paradox of lemmings is one of self-destruction. The explanation for this paradox remains a mystery to scientists, even after years of observation and study. The black widow spider paradox is one of being destructive to others. The black widow takes the phrase "you always hurt the one you love" literally.

At different times poor listeners behave like both lemmings and black widow spiders. They can be both self-destructive and destructive to others, even those they may love. In our workshops, the goal is to help participants discover ways to enhance their listening and improve their relationships through how they choose to listen. Effective listening can have positive, healing power. On the other hand, as with lemmings and black widow spiders, ineffective listening can damage and destroy relationships.

Listening as a Lethal Weapon

How does a poor listener behave like a lemming? Ineffective listening caused a fiery death when a power plant worker was told not to use an elevator because a fire had broken out five stories above. The worker didn't listen, entered the elevator, and was burned to death when the elevator shaft exploded.

Ineffective listeners can also behave like black widow spiders.

When an airline pilot misinterpreted instructions to detour around an active runway while taxiing at the Los Angeles International Airport, her crew and passengers were killed. The error led to a two-plane runway crash, causing numerous deaths and permanent injuries.

The primary cause of casualty in both of these cases, according to investigators, was human listening error. Fortunately for all of us, the results of most listening errors are less disastrous than these. Some listening failures cause only embarrassment, such as not remembering the name of a new acquaintance. Other listening errors cause minor inconvenience, such as missing a doctor's appointment or arriving at a friend's house for dinner on the wrong night. Whether the errors are life-threatening or annoying, ineffective listening damages family relationships, derails business negotiations, and destroys international ventures.

While Mother Nature's secrets about lemmings and black widow spiders remain a mystery, the secrets of effective listening are not as mysterious. But discovering the secrets of listening is not enough.

The Greatest Listening Paradox

Although there are many paradoxes surrounding listening behavior, perhaps the greatest is that *most of us admit we don't listen effectively and yet do little to improve.*[1] Of course, there are a number of other destructive behaviors that people are unwilling or unable to overcome such as excessive drinking, smoking, eating, or drug use. Consequently, at first glance, it might appear that the listening paradox is not so unusual. The difference lies in the fact that listening errors and breakdowns are often perceived as trivial or easy to forgive. The examples at the beginning of this chapter, however, emphasize the fact that listening breakdowns can be every bit as destructive to oneself and others as harmful addictions.

In our workshops we ask participants to rate themselves as listeners on a scale of 0 to 100. Most have never thought about rating themselves as listeners. They say it would have been easier if we'd asked them to rate themselves as public speakers, writers, golfers, or mathematicians. With these skills, they have a benchmark by which to compare their abilities. However, since listening is an internal process, most of us have never considered how well we listen. Take a moment, now to score yourself as a listener. On a scale from 0 to 100, how well do you listen:

- at home?   _____
- professionally?   _____

Most of us base our scores on what others have told us—"You're a good listener" or "You never remember anything that I say." When we ask participants for a numerical score we usually get scores in the range of 35 to 85, with the mean hovering around 60. Now, if your child were to bring home a 60 on a spelling test or you were to score a 60 on the written exam of a driving test, you would be less than pleased (and in the case of the driving test, barred from the road). Why is it that when we discover mistakes in how we listen, we do little or nothing to improve? Could it be that we rely on the dangerous assumption that we can listen well if we have to? Or is it that the negative consequences have not been great enough to force us to change?

Now that you have given yourself a listening score, take this exercise one step further. Consider how the most significant people in your life would rate you as a listener. Write down the score you think each of the following people would give you on the same 0 to 100 point scale.

- Best friend   _____
- Boss   _____
- Co-worker or peer   _____

- Direct report (if applicable)   ———
- Spouse/significant other/romantic partner
  (if applicable and if the spouse is not
  your best friend)   ———
- Children (if applicable/especially teenagers)   ———

Now compare the score you gave yourself with the scores you think others would give you. Are the scores higher, lower, or the same as compared to the score you gave yourself?

Through the years, our participants' scores usually follow the same pattern. We assume that our best friends would give us the highest scores (usually much higher than we rate ourselves). This makes sense: One reason we think of a person as our best friend is because they listen. Most of us also think that our bosses would rate us higher than we rate ourselves. Even if we don't agree with what our bosses say, most of us mask our true feelings and/or fake attention when we listen to them. One reason that we may demonstrate more effective listening behavior to a boss is because he or she has more power and influence over us.

Predictably, the scores we think our peers would give us are usually about the same as we give ourselves. In contrast, in most cases we believe that our direct reports or those individuals we supervise would rate us lower than we rate ourselves. Even if we do listen, many of us don't get credit for it because we don't always do what others ask. Many of us believe that another person is listening only if he or she agrees with us and/or does what we ask.

We usually think our spouse or long-term significant other would give us the lowest score. In fact, this score is often 20 to 30 points lower than the scores we give ourselves. After living with a person for a number of years, many of us get lazy as listeners. We may fake attention, assume that we know what the other person is about to say, or tune-out as a habit. It is interesting to note that many new relationships begin with a person seeking someone who understands and will listen to them.

Teenagers are another group of important people who we think may rate us lower than we rate ourselves. Similar to direct reports who don't think their bosses listen, children (especially teenagers) have goals that often conflict with those of their parents. Fortunately, as teenagers mature into young adults, the scores begin to go up.

Think for a moment about the skills that you have worked to improve. The list might include golf swings, tennis strokes, fishing casts, bridge strategies, and a host of other activities you've made priorities. Listening is the one skill that can improve relationships, health, wealth, and happiness more than any other, but it is also the one that few of us rarely make an effort to change. Instead, ineffective listening is a relationship liability that many of us choose to ignore.

Three Common Listening Pitfalls

In addition to the fact that *most of us admit we have done little to improve our listening effectiveness*, there are three common listening pitfalls that impact our relationships. Before considering these pitfalls, answer the following question:

- If you were in a room full of tarantulas, would you rather have the light on or off?

If you are like most people, you'd say, "ON!" Learning about these pitfalls turns the lights on.

■ The Do You Love Me? Pitfall.
Many of us give more listening energy to our work associates than to our loved ones. Yet, when we're asked what we value most—our families or jobs—most say our families.

Bill, a syndicated cartoonist working in Manhattan, told us that when he gets home after a full day at work and a two-hour commute, he's run out of gas. He feels guilty about not wanting to listen to his wife and children talk about their day's activities.

After a typical day on the job, few workers have energy saved for their families and friends. Think of a typical workday in your life. Do you spend energy listening carefully to peers, clients, and bosses, only to arrive home after work exhausted and too tired to listen patiently to your spouse, children, or significant other? You are not alone! Fortunately, there are concrete strategies to conserve and replenish listening energy that we will highlight in chapter 5.

■ The Oops, Sorry 'bout That! Pitfall.

Because listening is an internal process, it's hard to know if messages are getting through. Most of us believe that others understand our messages until something goes wrong. We described the tragedy of the two-plane crash in Los Angeles earlier. Federal investigators examining airplane mishaps identify listening errors and mechanical failures as two of the key contributors to airline accidents. They note that although airplane maintenance gets a lot of attention, major airlines could improve their records if listening effectiveness were emphasized throughout pilot training.

Even in our daily activities we fall victim to costly listening errors that go undetected until after the fact. Think back. Can you recall a recent listening error that caused someone close to you discomfort, embarrassment, pain, or financial loss? If so, does the phrase "Oops, sorry 'bout that" ring a bell?

■ The Not Seeing Is Not Believing Pitfall.

We've all had to prove that we can do more than one thing at a time, especially when it comes to listening.

61

Ralph, a teenager in North Dakota, infuriates his mother by playing computer games when she is trying to have a serious discussion. Ralph doesn't understand why his mother is making a big deal about it. He feels he is bright enough to play on the computer and listen at the same time.

Ralph is a member of Generation Y, those born in the late seventies and early eighties. Members of Generation Y, according to researchers, tend to pride themselves in being able to do several things at once. *Parallel processing* is the technical term used to describe this skill of listening and doing something else at the same time, which is nothing new but is increasingly common as our culture speeds up.

The problem is that, even if we can truly listen while doing something else, we may not get credit for it.[3] In most situations, listening success is not measured only in terms of comprehension, but in terms of *how connected* we feel with each other. To be effective listeners, we need to show that we are listening. Only through attentiveness and responsiveness can we listen—and convey we're listening.

Jump-starting Listening Improvement

Weight Watchers has spent years exploring ways to help participants follow suggestions for losing weight. They recently developed a "jump start" program in which participants could lose five to ten pounds very quickly. The program developers recognized that losing a few pounds quickly was a great motivator to help dieters continue the program. In our seminars and workshops we've incorporated this jump-start concept into personal listening improvement plans for our participants.

If you want to jump-start your listening skills, there is one technique that will give you immediate rewards. The technique was developed to overcome the obstacle identified in the "The Seeing Is Not Believing" paradox. It simply involves focusing on looking and sounding like you are listening to others. This technique applies in face-to-face interactions, meetings, and even lectures.

Looking Like a Good Listener

One of our favorite segments on *Saturday Night Live* featured the gold-chained, trendily dressed would-be playboy whose favorite expression was, "You look marvelous." His creed was, "It's not important what you do as long as you look good doing it." In listening, looking good is not everything, but it definitely counts. As we pointed out with Ralph of Generation Y, you may be listening but not get credit for it. If others don't believe you are listening because you're playing a computer game, signing papers, watching television, or looking at an attractive person walking by, then to them you aren't listening.

> Betty, a combined people- and action-oriented supervisor with an international bank, models her listening behavior after Wayne, her first boss. He was the best listener and manager she's ever known. On Betty's first day of work, Wayne gave his ground rules: "Betty, the key to our working relationship is good communication. I value you and what you have to offer. When you come into my office you'll have my undivided attention when I move whatever I'm working on to the side of my desk. You'll also know I've stopped listening when I move the work back to the center of my desk." He rarely moved his work to the center of his desk when someone was in his office.

Even though you may be able to repeat what others have said word-for-word, you still aren't perceived as really understanding or caring unless you look like you are listening. As the saying goes, people don't care how much you know until they know how much you care.

Show others you're listening by:

- using frequent eye contact
- leaning forward slightly
- nodding frequently
- giving nonverbal feedback often

Sounding Like a Good Listener

While most of our examples to this point have described face-to-face interactions, many conversations occur over the phone. When others can't see what you are doing, it becomes even more critical to use your voice to demonstrate interest and concern. At times, you may have to modify or even exaggerate your typical responses to let others know you are listening. However, there are times when exaggeration is not effective. In working with 911 operators, we emphasize how important it is for them to demonstrate effective listening through the calmness and control of their voices.

It was almost midnight when Bettina received a call from a distraught man saying, "I'm going into insulin shock and I can't find my syringe!" Maintaining a calm voice, Bettina began asking specific questions about his name, location, time since his last injection, entry into the house, etc. After getting his name and other critical information, she worked to keep her voice calm and to stay connected verbally to Mr. Thompson. Keeping in mind her voice tone, volume, and inflection, Bettina related that the ambulance was on the way, emphasized that she would stay on the line until it arrived, and asked questions that required Mr. Thompson to respond every few seconds.

In most phone conversations, people want auditory markers or reminders that another person is listening.

Sound like an effective listener by:

- using frequent verbal responses that show you are listening
- increasing your volume slightly
- varying pitch and inflection
- speaking a little more quickly

Immediate Rewards

Most of us have lots of opportunities each day to practice these suggestions. As we begin to look and sound more and more like we are listening, we'll reap at least two different rewards.

The first is that our friends, relatives, and co-workers will believe that we care for and respect them. This action in turn usually leads to developing closer and higher quality relationships.

We asked one of our time-oriented clients to share what changes he noticed at work after we had coached him on how to give more direct eye contact and specific follow-up responses to what others said. After he related several success stories, we probed about his home life. With tears in his eyes, he said, "I asked my wife if she'd noticed any changes since I'd been working with you. She turned to me and said, "I think you love me more than you used to. . . ."

The second reward may surprise you. Research has shown that when we consciously try to put our body and mind in a positive listening mode—our listening effectiveness actually increases. The concept of body and mind-set "readiness" is the key to this benefit.[4] We are conditioned to look and sound a certain way when we are listening at our best. When we consciously mirror how we look and sound when we are listening attentively, our listening effectiveness improves at the same time.

Throughout the remainder of this book, we'll suggest several additional ways to overcome listening obstacles. However, by looking and sounding like a good listener, you have a jump-start toward listening improvement.

REFERENCES

1. K. W. Watson, and L. L. Barker (1992). Listener assumptions: Guidelines for trainers. *Training & Development*, 15–17.
2. L. K. Steil, L. L. Barker and K. W. Watson (1983). *Effective Listening: Key To Your Success*. New York: McGraw-Hill, Inc.
3. K. W. Watson and L. L. Barker (1993). Eight dangerous assumptions speakers make about listeners. *The Toastmaster Magazine*, 17–19.
4. N. R. Carlson (1990). *Psychology: The Science of Behavior* (3rd Ed.). Boston: Allyn and Bacon.

5

Listening Is Not a Spectator Sport: Limited Energy Supply and Listener Burnout

"Everybody's lying these days, but it doesn't matter because nobody's listening."

—LIEBERMAN'S LAW

Shelly shuffles into our office and collapses in a chair. "I can't take it anymore! Last week I had to listen to everyone complain about getting a new computer system. Now this week everyone is sharing war stories about how slow it used to be without computers. I'm sick and tired of listening to these crybabies!"

We can all relate to listener fatigue. In our work with families and business clients, we've found that continuous listening to others takes its toll on relationships. When we listen too hard for too long, we experience listening burnout. Most of us don't realize the need to replenish our supply of listening energy. In fact, instead of renewing our supplies, we often allow valuable listening energy to slip away.

As Theodore enters Sandy's office, she unconsciously begins focusing attention on his problems. She has just come out of a long meeting and is already low on listening energy. Before she knows it, her listening tank is nearly empty. Theodore senses that Sandy is becoming frustrated and doesn't know why. He feels she is not interested in his concerns—although that is not the case. Now he's less willing to open up to her, and she doesn't understand why.

Our ability to fulfill daily demands with enough listening energy depends on our success in conserving our resources throughout the day. When job demands are high, we may have little or no listening energy left for family members and friends.

Listening Burnout: Listening Harder Isn't Listening Smarter

Listener burnout is a real problem in today's workplace. Rosetta, one of our seminar participants, shared the following account of a typical workday.

On Monday morning, after a good night's sleep, Rosetta had a full tank of listening energy. As the day began, her supply started to diminish. During routine and pleasant breakfast interactions with Joshua, her nine-year-old, little energy was used. However, an argument with the school bus driver erupted, and her listening supply began to go down. She got to the processing plant a few minutes late, after losing a fight for a parking space. As she entered her office her phone was ringing and co-workers began requesting her time, knowledge, and listening energy.

By 10 A.M. Rosetta, by her own admission, had used about half of her available listening energy. By noon she estimated she had used about 70 percent of the energy she started with. In the afternoon her boss talked with her about her lack of concentration, frustration, and impatience. His observations prompted Rosetta to attend our listening seminar.

Those of us who work on staggered schedules, night shifts, or who describe ourselves as "night people" may have different patterns than Rosetta described. Whatever our schedule, interactions and daily pressures work to deplete listening energy reserves, which can lead to listening burnout.

Maximizing Listening Energy

An essential tool to help avoid listening burn out is the process of **self-monitoring,** which, in this context, is the process of "listening to" and "observing" oneself. One use for self-monitoring involves regularly observing how much energy you have to listen

---

The process of self-monitoring includes three steps:

1. Making a commitment to "look out for" or watch for the behavior you want to observe
2. Catching yourself using or demonstrating the behavior
3. Making a choice whether to change or continue the behavior you observed

---

When self-monitoring, the goal is to be unobtrusive. You don't want your observations to interfere with your interactions. These observations can help you make more productive listening choices.

> Amy, an advertising executive, had had a grueling day of phone calls and client meetings. Noticing her fatigue, she decided to listen to soothing music while taking a hot bath. When she saw her mother's car as she was about to pull into her driveway, her heart dropped. Through self-monitoring and observation, Amy realized she didn't have sufficient energy to listen to her mom's problems at the moment. Instead of going home immediately, she drove around the block and stopped at a local coffee shop. There she ordered a latte, got an energy boost, and relaxed for a few minutes before going home.

By self monitoring, Amy made a conscious choice about to whom, what, and when she wanted to listen. If we don't make conscious choices, we are influenced by whatever distractions, interruptions, or individuals happen to enter our listening world.

Listening Energy Reservoirs

What is listening energy? Why is it that Jane finds it easy to answer all of her three-year-old's "why" questions early in the day and is ready to scream when asked the same question at 4:00 in the afternoon? Why does Andrea respond with compassion to wisecracks from her juvenile court wards at the beginning of the week and snap back by the end of the workday on Friday? Why does Karen find her mind wandering during executive committee meetings on some days and not others? There are differences in when and how we can listen that correspond to the quality of energy we have in reserve.[2] We expend *physical, emotional,* and *intellectual energy* all day long. Good listening requires all three forms of energy.

> A good example occurred when Monique had the flu. Her body needed rest to heal. A poor patient in the best of circumstances and with a major project due, Monique was determined to complete a report. Unfortunately, the fever and chills took too much energy for her to think clearly for extended periods. She made a few calls and tried to concentrate and then would forget what she'd just heard. She didn't have enough high-level energy required for thinking or listening. If that wasn't frustrating enough, her emotional energy was depleted as well. Phone calls with get-well wishes, appreciated during normal circumstances, felt intrusive and inconvenient. She found it difficult to focus or remember what others were saying and got frustrated when she heard herself responding irritably.

It's important to note that even though Monique had sufficient energy to hear, she did not have enough energy to listen completely. Unfortunately, there's no way for someone else to know if we're out of energy to listen well. If we want to ensure meaningful interactions, it's critical to self-monitor our own listening energy levels to assess our ability to listen.

When emotional or intellectual listening energy is low, it is natural for nervousness, irritability, or hostility to surface. Think about how difficult it is to listen when you are tired and how easy it is for senseless arguments, frustrations, and pouting sessions to occur. Just before bedtime most energy for problem solving, clear thinking, and remembering has slipped away. This is one reason that research reports suggest the most happily married couples agree to avoid discussing sensitive issues when their energy is low[3] (some say after 10:00 P.M.).

"The practice of simple awareness is impossible without control of attention. Attention is to awareness as the oil in a lamp is to its flame. While there is oil in the lamp, the flame persists. Once the oil is exhausted, the flame goes out. Control of attention is the one function that man [woman] possesses which may be said to confer on him [her] a certain amount of free will. He [she] can 'direct his [her] attention.' But his [her] power to do this depends upon his [her] processing a certain kind of energy the supply of which is limited. Each day, on awakening, he [she] has just so much of this energy, as a battery, after being charged, contains just so much electrical potential. His [her] inner work each day depends on the conservation of this energy. Once it has been squandered, it is hard to replace." —R. S. DeRopp, *The Master Game*

Your Listening Reserve Tank

The first Volkswagen Beetle, manufactured in the 1940s, included a reserve tank as a feature for use when the primary gas tank ran out. These reserve tanks have saved many motorists from walking down deserted roads at night after running out of gas. Similarly, our listening energy tank has a reserve that can be tapped in emergency situations. The reserve tank kicks in when a sudden crisis demands our attention or when there is motivation to listen, even if we are out of energy in our primary tank. Unfortunately, however, the reserve energy doesn't guarantee that we can listen better—just that we are willing to pay attention.

Eric told us that his spouse became angry after he had given only half-hearted attention to her conversation during dinner. His wife, Joan, had been talking to her mother and she reported some of the highlights of the conversation. During dinner the phone rang. Eric answered the phone and began talking and listening intently to one of his fishing buddies. The talk centered on a successful trip Eric had missed. Joan felt hurt when Eric was willing to listen to his friend but not to her.

What happened was completely understandable from a listening point of view, although Joan might not like the explanation. At the dinner table, Eric had very little energy to give away. But, when a topic interested him a lot, he was willing to let the reserve tank kick in and spend his extra energy to listen. (In essence, adrenaline was released into the bloodstream.) Most of us can recall similar incidents when we were willing to spend energy to listen because of high interest or during a crisis condition. Although we were almost exhausted or out of primary listening energy, we mustered a so-called second wind.

Listening Energy Sappers

Americans learned during the energy crisis of the '70s that conserving fuel is as important as finding new fuel sources. This principle also applies to solving listening energy crises. The most severe drain on listening energy comes from what we call **energy sappers.** Some of the most common listening energy sappers are internal sappers such as worry, anxiety, or physical fatigue. Other sappers from outside us include conflict situations, city noises, or time demands. People can be the biggest energy drain. Similar to "brain drain," people sapping occurs when we react to emotional words in a conversation or deal with overbearing or selfish people. Sapping, especially in professions with high people contact, occurs throughout the day.

Cherise rushed to be on time for a 4:00 P.M. parent-teacher conference. Charlie, her six-year-old son, had been having some reading problems and the teacher asked Cherise to meet her Wednesday after school. Traffic was bad and there was a fender bender on 10th Avenue, so she had to detour several blocks to reach the school. When she arrived the children were just leaving their classrooms—noisy and agitated. The school bell was ringing—so loud that it hurt Cherise's ears. To top it off, when she reached the classroom she saw six other mothers sitting in line, ahead of her, to talk with the teacher. She knew that if she didn't complete the conference by 5:00 P.M., she would be late to pick up her teenage daughter, Kelli, from softball practice at the community center. When she finally was called in to see Miss Delvaney it was 4:55 P.M. Miss Delvaney immediately blamed Cherise for not helping Charlie with his homework. Needless to say, the conference went south from there.

Cherise's listening energy had been totally sapped before their meeting. (It's a good bet that Miss Delvaney, as a first grade teacher and with multiple conferences, also had experienced a few people sappers of her own before meeting with Cherise.)

Energy sappers don't have to affect us negatively. But we often allow them to. The key is to keep an eye out (actually, an ear out) for sappers and head them off whenever possible. Once again, the process of self-monitoring is critical. As you become more aware of the importance of energy in effective listening, you can make strides to conserve energy, restore lost energy, and build new energy when you need it. Keep in mind that people- and content-oriented listeners are usually willing to expend more listening energy than action- or time-oriented listeners. They don't necessarily have more energy, but they are willing to dip into their listening reservoir more frequently.

Six Ways to Refuel Listening Energy

How can you get and keep sufficient energy to listen—and be heard—more effectively, even in the face of relentless energy sappers? Here are six strategies.

1. **Have a Plan.** Planning ahead for conversations helps conserve listening energy. One of our workshop participants, Greg, took this advice to heart with favorable results. With a booming keynote speaking business, 80 percent of his time was spent in marketing and booking engagements. As a general rule, he planned casual and relatively easy-to-deal-with people and conversations during the first and last thirds of his telephone day. Important, critical, challenging, or stressful people or meetings were scheduled, whenever possible, when his energy was at its highest—usually in the middle third of his day. Although his energy was high early in the day, Greg found his potential clients hadn't cleared out internal noise and distractions at the beginning of a day. He found their concentration best during late morning and early afternoon conference calls.

   When planning get-togethers with friends or business colleagues, think about what kind of listening energy will be required. Schedule relatively easy-to-deal-with but important topics early in the day, critical and highly important topics during the middle, and less important, noncontroversial topics during the last part of the day.

   Our listening energy ebbs and flows during meetings. Effective listeners remember the Listening Energy Rule of Thirds. During the first third of the meeting, your energy level will be at its highest. However, you may be distracted somewhat by previous events or conversations just preceding the meeting. During the second third of the meeting, your listening energy will still be high, and you should find it easy to concentrate on the critical topics and issues. During the last third of the meeting your energy supply will be lower, and you may begin to be distracted by thinking about what you need to do immediately after the meeting ends. Realizing your typical listening energy expenditure during meetings can help you pace yourself and have some energy left at the end of the meeting to make important decisions and contributions.

Making a plan to listen can apply to personal or intimate conversations with friends, spouses, or children.

> Noticing that his wife's listening energy was low, Sam made a mental note to keep the conversation light. He asked questions about how work went, what the children were doing, and what she wanted to do over the weekend. He delayed mentioning his desire to join an additional bowling league. He knew the timing was bad to bring up sensitive, controversial, or stressful issues. Even though he will discuss the issue, he strategically delayed the topic until she has more energy. He wants to make sure they both have high-quality energy for listening and talking.

2. **Watch Energy Sappers.** As mentioned earlier, troublesome people and events sap listening energy. The best way to conserve energy is to identify what sappers take the most energy. The following checklist gives you a way to determine where you're losing valuable listening energy.

Energy Sappers Checklist

In each category, you may have sappers of your own to add; this is especially true of personal sappers.

Internal Sappers

——— Worry and anxiety

——— Emotional identification with topic, point of view, or position

——— Defensiveness

——— Hunger/thirst

——— Time of day (morning, afternoon, or night person)

——— Sickness or physical fatigue

External Sappers

——— Conflict situations

——— Visual or auditory noise

——— Sensory overload

——— Interpersonal friction

——— Multiple tasks to complete with a limited amount of time

——— Trying to outline everything in a talk (note taking)

People Sappers

——— Getting distracted by someone's verbal style or appearance

——— Reacting to emotional words in a conversation

——— Dealing with overbearing or selfish associates

——— Dealing with people who don't value your time

Personal Sappers [add your own]

———

———

The best way to decrease or eliminate energy sappers is to set specific goals (preferably in writing) to avoid or reduce such energy drains. Keeping the list in your appointment book or in your desk reminds you to watch out for their negative effects.

Whenever a sapper is present, you can take steps to head it off or reduce the negative outcomes. With people who tend to drain your energy, you may schedule interactions with them at times when your energy is high. You might even find ways to reduce the number of face-to-face interactions with such people and use written messages or electronic mail, if appropriate.

3. **Know Your Body Clock.** The example earlier in this chapter concerning Rosetta's workday suggested that she was basically a "day person."

> Vali, on the other hand, prefers to start her day about noon and work late into the evening. On those days when she's forced to attend early rehearsals with her band, she can't hit some of the high notes and her voice doesn't reflect the power and emotions she has when rested. Her singing (and listening) energy tends to increase as the day unfolds. Vali is a classic "night person."

When you are aware of your typical daily cycles of energy, you can plan when (and when not) to engage in important listening interactions and events. If you are not sure whether you are more of a day or night person, chart your energy levels at different times throughout the day for three days in a row.[4] Of course, we all vary in energy levels from time to time; what we're trying to establish is your *typical* body energy cycles. Once you believe that you understand your body energy cycle, you can better plan listening events to coincide with your highest levels of energy.

4. **Set an Alarm.** Alarm clocks remind us to check our listening energy supply. Although we're primarily thinking of the alarm clock as an analogy, hourly beeps on some watches or clocks can help remind us to monitor our listening energy supply at the moment. The concept of setting alarms extends beyond actual clocks. Such reminders as notes inside your desk, a question mark written on a calendar, mirror, or other location you view frequently, or even a framed quotation or picture, can serve as a reminder to check your supply.

> Xavier, a project manager for a construction company, developed a screen saver for his office computer with a series of multi colored spinning and rotating ears. When he looked at the screen it reminded him to check his listening energy at that moment. When he realized that he was getting low, he took a break and walked through the courtyard to a coffee shop on the other side of the building to replenish his energy supply.

5. **Stop the Show.** The old adage in show business that "the show must go on" doesn't apply in most listening settings. In actuality, as discussed in Chapter 1, listeners can usually control most communication outcomes. There are at least four ways you, as a listener, can "stop the show."

   • **Ask for a listening break.** Either be direct or manufacture a reason to get out of the listening role for a short period. Reasonable requests like asking to be excused to go the restroom, get a drink, or make an important call are hard for most people to refuse.

Mel realized that her husband, Mark, expected her to go over some financial issues before dinner. She observed her energy supply and realized that if they began the discussion now, it would probably lead to disagreements and frustration. She asked Mark if he would mind waiting to go over the finances until after dinner, because she would be more focused. Mark somewhat reluctantly agreed to postpone the discussion. When their dinner was over both were in a happier and more relaxed mood and the discussion went well.

- **Request down time.** As simple as this suggestion sounds, most of us don't take the direct approach and ask our friends or loved ones to help us renew our energy for listening.

When Frank, a hospital director, gets home from work, he routinely goes into his room and changes his clothes. His family has agreed not to "bombard" him with questions or information until he comes out of the room in his casual clothes.

If, like Frank, you realize that you need some decompression time after a hard day to replenish your energy supply, let that fact be known. You may have to remind your family and friends of your needs from time to time, but chances are they will do their best to help you—if you are willing to ask for their help and support.

- **Adjourn the conversation or meeting early.** This might mean postponing some issues for discussion. Another possibility is to ask the group to eliminate relatively unimportant items from the agenda.

> Frederika is director of a small group. Their meeting to select the next musical had gone on for over two hours and there were still several items on the agenda that needed to be addressed. Although there was frustration about not finishing, Frederika persuaded the group to adjourn the meeting and reschedule a "stand-up" meeting on Sunday afternoon. At the stand-up meeting no one sits down—and this helps move the group through the agenda more quickly. The Sunday afternoon meeting only lasted thirty minutes and all the issues were resolved to the group's satisfaction.

The goal is to stop the interaction before listening energy levels become too low. In some instances you may notice others' energy levels getting low, rather than your own. It is a good idea to suggest adjourning the meeting or interaction early for everyone's sake.

- **Openly admit you're tired.** If appropriate, ask others to bear with you and move as quickly as possible to "the bottom line."

> Mildred realized that she was drifting in and out of her conversation with Ron. Ron was enthusiastically talking about his upcoming skiing trip to Aspen. Although Mildred usually enjoyed hearing about Ron's plans, she had had a hectic day at work and had developed a slight headache. "I really want to hear about the trip." Mildred sighed. "But, I'm too bushed now to enjoy all the details. How about

meeting me for lunch tomorrow and I'll have more energy to listen." Ron appreciated Mildred's openness and readily accepted the lunch date.

If your request is made in a sincere, nonhostile manner, chances are people will understand and perhaps even empathize with you. If the other person reacts in a hostile manner or refuses to get to the point, you may have to draw on your reserve listening tank. Our experience is that once people realize that you don't have adequate energy to listen, they will attempt to accommodate your request to end the meeting or interaction as quickly as possible.

6. **Rebuild Energy.** This method includes finding effective and efficient ways to build or replenish energy that has been drained throughout the day. Many of these techniques are useful for general stress management as well as for building listening energy.

Change the Environment
- Take a break
- Vary your routine
- Go outdoors
- Change rooms

Reduce Office/Home/Car Stimuli
- Go to lunch alone
- Close your eyes
- Drive in the car without the radio
- Dim the lights

Create a New Frame of Mind
- Listen to soothing music
- Visualize a serene picture

- Take a nap
- Read for pleasure
- Write a note or letter
- Touch someone or be touched by someone
- Find someone who will listen to you

Do Something Physical
- Take a walk
- Plan stretch or stand-up breaks during meetings
- Exercise or use isometrics

Each of these suggestions alone or in combination can help regenerate precious energy and reduce listening burnout. We just have to take the time to do it.

REFERENCES

1. K. Paulin and P. J. Canonie (1983). It's time to listen to ourselves. *Effective Listening Quarterly*, 3, 1; S. C. Rhodes (1989). Listening and intrapersonal communication. In C. V. Roberts and K. W. Watson (eds.), *Intrapersonal Communication Processes* (pp. 547–569). New Orleans: SPECTRA, Inc.
2. R. D. Halley (1997). *And Then I Was Surprised by What You Said.* Columbia, MO: KAIA Publishing, p. 19.
3. M. A. Fizpatrick and F. S. Wamboldt (1990). When it is all said and done? Toward an integration of intrapersonal and interpersonal models of marital and family communication. *Communication Research, 17*, 421–430.
4. B. Gittelson (1976). *Biorhythm: A Personal Science.* New York: Warner Books.

6

I'm Okay, But I'm Not So Sure About You: How Poor Listening Damages Relationships

> Listening is an attitude of the heart, a genuine desire to be with another which both attracts and heals.
>
> —J. ISHAM

Time-oriented Maude paced the lobby, looking toward the door every few minutes expecting her date to arrive. She felt embarrassed when the maître d' asked for the third time, "Would you like to be seated?" Finally, she dialed Derek's cell phone number. He answered the phone, saying, "Where are you?" She answered, in a huff, "I'm at Mike's on the Avenue, where you told me to be." He responded, "Well, I'm at Mike Anderson's, where we agreed to meet!" After making excuses, they hung up, each blaming the other for not listening.

As noted in Chapter 2, listening usually goes unnoticed until something goes wrong. It is only after missing an important meeting or forgetting to return a call that we begin to consider whether we listened well. When confronted about poor listening habits by friends, spouses, or colleagues, we tend to get defensive or make excuses. In fact, most of us can easily list what gets in the way of our listening efforts. Who hasn't thought or said:

"The reason I didn't hear you was because the telephone was ringing off the hook."
"I thought I got what you said, but I think the people in the office were too noisy."
"How could anyone listen to a speaker that boring?"
"When she started talking with that monotone and slow pace, my mind started to wander."

While there are reasons for not listening, barriers to listening effectively, different listener preferences, and making excuses keep us from overcoming them. Even when we do have a good excuse and apologize for our listening mistakes, relationships suffer when we forget what others say or act like what they're talking about is unimportant. Do the following comments sound familiar?

"I told you that last week."
"I forgot."
"I asked you to get whole milk for the baby, not skim milk!"
"If you'd been listening the first time, I wouldn't have to repeat myself."

Irritating Listening Habits

Ladies' Home Journal subscribers were asked: "If you could improve one thing about your husbands what would it be?" Out of all the possibilities, the number one change women wanted was for their husbands to be better listeners. Fifty-seven percent wished their husbands were better listeners as compared to 46 percent wanting a husband who helped out more around the house and 40 percent wishing their husbands made more money.[1]

In our workshops participants often share accounts about why their marriages or relationships failed. Most talk about not being understood, valued, or heard. In disintegrating relationships and over time, partners develop irritating listening habits and stop listening to each other.

> Clay and Elaine had recently started seeing a marriage counselor. During one session, the counselor asked Elaine what she wanted from Clay as a husband. As Elaine responded, Clay made a face and started shaking his head. The counselor stopped Elaine and asked Clay what he was thinking. Clay said, "I just know what she's going to say. She always says the same thing, she wants me to ask questions about her day, stop watching so much television, stay off the computer, bla-bla-bla." Then, Elaine started shaking her head and said, "He always does this to me. He thinks he knows what I'm going to say before I say it—sometimes he's right, but most of the time I feel like he doesn't even know me. Why can't he let me finish what I'm saying?"

Finishing someone else's sentences or interrupting conversations causes frustration and is often associated with some action- and time-oriented listeners. When we think we know what a friend is about to say, we may interject without allowing the person to finish and miss valuable information. These irritating behaviors, when conditioned and reinforced over time, can seriously damage relationships.

As researchers, we have been curious about which poor listening habits are most harmful in relationships. By collecting data from sem-

---

Top Ten Irritating Listening Habits

1. Interrupting the speaker.
2. Not looking at the speaker.
3. Rushing the speaker and making him feel that he's wasting the listener's time.
4. Showing interest in something other than the conversation.
5. Getting ahead of the speaker and finishing her thoughts.
6. Not responding to the speaker's requests.
7. Saying, "Yes, but . . . ," as if the listener has made up his mind.
8. Topping the speaker's story with "That reminds me . . ." or "That's nothing, let me tell you about . . ."
9. Forgetting what was talked about previously.
10. Asking too many questions about details.

---

inar participants, students, clients, and colleagues we've compiled a list of irritating listening habits. Above are the top ten.

Are there other annoying habits you would like to add? Are you guilty of any of these habits? When we are honest with ourselves most of us will admit that we have been guilty of practicing these or other irritating listening habits in the past.

Hurting the Ones You Love

In Chapter 4 we pointed out that we often display our worst listening habits with the ones we care the most about. Some poor listening habits are obvious and others, while just as harmful, aren't.

Stella and her sister-in-law, Renee, went to the track to get some exercise and visit after not seeing each other for six months. Renee asked Stella how her daughter liked her part-time job at McDonald's. Renee, a true extrovert, interrupted her twice as she told her about her daughter's training program. When Stella took a breath after saying, "She is pretty tired now because . . ." Immediately, Renee jumped in and said, "Getting up early is hard on her and she really likes her sleep." Frustrated, Stella said, "No, that wasn't what I was going to say. If you'd let me finish. . . ." Renee looked puzzled and hurt after Stella's outburst.

Eventually, Stella stopped sharing what was going on in her daughter's life. Rather than having to start over or correcting her sister-in-law, she disengaged.

When someone interrupts, we get frustrated and lose our desire to communicate. Responses that break into our words cause us to lose our train of thought. While the irritating listening habits outlined above are evident to other people, some of the most damaging poor listening habits are hidden from view.

The Sounds of Silence

Take a few minutes to compete this exercise:

1. Set a timer on your watch or microwave for thirty seconds.
2. For these thirty seconds, close your eyes and just listen to all the sounds in your environment.
3. After thirty seconds, get a sheet of paper and write down every sound that you heard.

Welcome back. You should have been able to list at least five different sounds. Your list may have included: air conditioning or furnace fans, outside traffic, a plane overhead, rustling of paper or clothing, footsteps in the hall, doors shutting, elevators dinging, your own breathing, telephones ringing, printers/machinery sounds, voices, music, or nature's music such as birds or crickets chirping. Depending on your listening environment, your list of sounds will vary.

You may not have been aware of most of these sounds prior to this exercise. By focusing your awareness on such sounds you were able to identify them and classify them as important or inconsequential.

Were there any sounds that you overlooked? Did you, for example, hear your own inner voice? If you listed your voice first, good for you. Even though our inner voice is the loudest sound we hear, most of us are unaware of how it distracts us when we're in conversations with others.

Throughout the day, our inner voice never stops talking. Even during this exercise, your inner voice probably made comments such as:

"This is a long thirty seconds."
"Why would the authors ask us to do something like this?"
"There are more sounds than I thought."
or
"I don't hear anything."

Your inner voice is the loudest sound in your world, and it often gets in the way of your relationships with others.

While inner voices can serve as a distraction and hinder relationships, they are important. Our inner voices help us monitor our interactions with ourselves and others, but sometimes the inner voice SCREAMS when it needs to WHISPER, INTERRUPTS when it needs to WAIT or ARGUES when it needs to REFLECT.

Quieting the inner voice long enough to really listen to others is a

---

Your inner voice may:

- hinder you from remembering names during introductions;
- encourage you to rush to a response ("the Great Comeback") before people finish their thoughts;
- jump to other topics and thoughts because of emotional trigger words or associations;
- block information from getting through when it is inconsistent with your past experience.

---

challenge. The key to regulating our inner voice is to work from an "other-centered" rather than "self-centered" listening perspective. As Steven Covey, author of *The 7 Habits of Highly Effective People*, writes: "Seek first to understand, then to be understood."[2]

The Impact of Poor Listening Habits

It is easier to notice how troublesome another person's listening habits are than it is for us to identify what gets in the way of our own listening effectiveness. Keep in mind that the strengths and weaknesses associated with your individual listener preferences may be troublesome to others. Unless pointed out, most habits become a routine part of the ways we interact. Habits are:

H—highly
A—automated
B—behaviors
I—intensified over
T—time.

In other words, with ongoing practice, we reinforce the way we choose to listen. Unfortunately, many of us are practicing bad habits that have become difficult to change.

Yielding to Distractions

Concentrating as a listener means staying focused on what another person is saying. When we are drawn to distractions rather than the person with whom we are communicating, we lose focus. Some distractions (music, loud voices, office machines, etc.) are noticeable; others, such your inner voice, may not be noticeable until there is a listening mistake.

> During breakfast, Kerry reminded her Dad about her last home game. As she talked, her Dad, Wayne, read the paper, slurped coffee at the sink, and jotted notes about his first sales call. When Kerry finished, Wayne gave her a quick hug and said, "I'll see you at the game."
>
> Wayne knew he was in deep trouble when he got to the high school gym and the doors were locked. He'd promised to show up today after missing three home games in a row. He thought Kerry had said the game was at 4:00 o'clock, but no one was around. Wayne started thinking, "I thought I was listening this morning, but I had so much on my mind. Why is it that I never miss a business appointment, but always get the kids' games messed up?"

Wayne knew that his daughter was going to be disappointed. He also knew that she would probably attribute how well he listened to how much he cared. Failing to remember commitments or listen effectively communicates that the other person isn't valued or important. We have all been guilty of forgetting something that was important. A

To control internal and external distractions:

- Remove or reduce distractions by turning off TVs and machines
- Sit or move in close range of your partner
- Minimize interruptions by finding a private environment
- Take notes
- Look at your partner frequently
- Be rested before beginning to listen

---

friend of ours used to say that the mind is as slippery as an eel. The goal is to find ways to hold on to ideas and information as long as possible.

Daydreaming

You may have seen the Federal Express commercial with one of the world's fastest talkers, John "Mighty Mouth" Moschitta, speaking at five hundred words per minute. For a limited time, people can muster enough listening energy to comprehend information at such a fast rate. Since most of us usually speak at one hundred twenty-five to one hundred fifty words per minute, we can listen at a much faster rate than others speak.[3] When others speak too slowly, we get in the habit of daydreaming or doodling rather than using the time to our advantage.

Most listeners fade in and out of conversations. The attention span

---

As a listener, use extra thought-speed time by:

- anticipating what a speaker is going to say next,
- summarizing what you have just heard, and
- evaluating the information.

---

of the average adult is between ten and twenty seconds without concentrated effort.[4] Most of us check in and out of conversations so often that we forget we are doing it. While we may look like we are listening, our minds may be thousands of miles away, focused on other matters large and small.

Even the best listeners have trouble maintaining interest in some conversations and/or lectures. If, however, we get in the habit of wasting the advantage of being able to listen faster than others can speak, we may miss valuable insights and discount relationships.

Becoming Overly Emotional

> Feeling a lump in her breast, Chris made an appointment to see her gynecologist, Dr. Gardner. Two days after the mammogram, the doctor's nurse called and told Chris that Dr. Gardner wanted her to schedule a follow-up exam. When Chris began to ask questions, the nurse kindly replied, "I'm sorry, but Dr. Gardner will have to answer your questions personally. Would you like for her to call you?" At that moment Chris stopped listening. Instead, out of fear, she started listening to her own inner voice as it began asking, "What's wrong with me? Do I have cancer? Will I have to have a mastectomy?" As the nurse continued talking, Chris missed everything she said.

When emotions, like the ones Chris felt, take over they tend to override logic and shut down our listening processes. This is one reason that when you realize a person is in an emotionally negative state of mind (angry, depressed, jealous, etc.), it is best to avoid talking until after the person has calmed down. Remember that negative emotions diminish a person's ability to listen. It's as if the emotions have a "will of their own." Sometimes we are aware we are reacting emotionally—

but feel we can do nothing to regain control. Through self-monitoring practice it is possible to become more aware of initial emotional triggers and head them off before they get us off track.

Shifting Attention to Ourselves

> Gunther always had to have the last word. If his co-workers talked about a local weekend fishing trip they enjoyed, he "had to" top their story by bragging on about a trophy marlin he caught in Australia. If his boss complained about having to stay at the office the night before until 7 P.M., Gunther "had to" explain that, although he left early, he worked at home until midnight.

We've all known and disliked people like Gunther. They appear to have a compulsion to play the "I can top that" game. The term "one-up-manship" is also used to describe this type of activity. The psychological basis for this competitive behavior is beyond the scope of our research. However, when topping someone else's story becomes a listening habit (actually a response habit) it can damage relationships and destroy potential friendships.

Talking Too Much

Larry Barker, one of this book's authors, was featured on an ABC *20/20* segment entitled "Excessive Talking."[5] Two situations were highlighted. One involved a woman who failed to maintain long-term romantic relationships because of her need to talk. In the other scenario, Larry worked as a leadership coach to help a manager learn to stop talking long enough to listen to and learn from his direct reports. Through the coaching relationship the manager identified how to ask questions without interrupting the response, look for cues of disinterest,

---

Keep in Mind:

- The more you talk the less you listen, and the more you talk the less others will listen
- When you talk too much it is just as hard to remember all you said as it is to remember what others said

---

present his ideas more concisely, and ask for help in becoming less over-bearing.

This manager and others we have worked with professionally now know that talking too much and too often turns others off. When you want to impress others and appear more powerful, learn to say less.[6] In fact, research shows that people who talk more than 80 percent of the time are not well liked.[7]

Managing Listening Expectations

Before leaving irritating behaviors, we need to emphasize that some of these behaviors may be necessary for a person's role and/or responsibility. Judges, for example, work to display impartiality when listening to testimony in the courtroom by maintaining blank facial expressions. In fact, some judges actually place mirrors in front of them on the bench to make sure they are displaying a neutral facial expression so as not to sway the jury. Similarly, detectives who are interrogating suspects often try to mask their true feelings. They may even interrupt suspects intentionally to intimidate them and keep them off balance. Negotiators, lawyers, mediators, and corrections officers also may consciously engage in irritating habits to achieve specific goals.

The listening habits we are concerned about are the ones that affect our interactions with others. When bosses, for example, continually ignore their employees' input they may inhibit suggestions or the sharing of ideas. Similarly, teenagers report that they stop sharing what they're thinking and feeling with most adults. When asked why, they claim that adults tune out whenever a point of view is different from their own. If we want to keep channels of communication open, we should take a look at our own irritating listening behaviors.

> Stella was thrilled to have a chance to spend her vacation with her best friend, Nancy. Since they hadn't seen each other in six months, Nancy rented a beach house away from everything for long walks and talks. Stella was surprised when Nancy arrived with her computer and fax machine. Nancy failed to tell Stella that the only way that she'd gotten off was to promise her boss that she'd finish a real estate deal by phone. When Nancy was beeped for the second time during the first hour, Stella got irritated.

Try to think about how you might have felt in a similar situation. Since others can't read our minds, they might perceive our inattention, interruptions, and distractions as an indication of how much we value them. Good listeners and communicators learn to avoid misperception when possible. You might explain to the person in your office, for example, why it was important to take a phone call with a customer who had been trying to reach you for three days. When we acknowledge the other person's feelings and explain our behavior, others are often more tolerant and accepting.

"Everyone thinks of changing the world, but no one thinks of changing himself."

—Leo Tolstoy

Changing Listening Habits

"Okay" you say, "I confess that I have some listening habits that need some work. And, yes, my listening preferences sometimes get in the way of how I listen to others. What's the next step?" To change listening habits you need a "TIP."

The TIP stands for:

T—training
I—incentive and
P—practice

Training

You're getting training in listening through reading this book. Here are a few ways to get the most from what you read:

Tip #1: Verify listening suggestions through your own experience. Don't try to implement ideas that don't make sense to you.

> Rob attended one of our seminars in Boston and was one of the more attentive participants. He took notes and made an action plan to change some of his ineffective listening habits. About a month after the seminar he called our office and said he was having some problems. He explained that he was working on self-monitoring, but every time he began to observe himself, it interfered with his conversation and he stopped listening. Eventually he got frustrated.

We reviewed some of the principles of self-monitoring in Chapter 5, including the concept that the goal is to remain a "detached" observer and not pass immediate judgment on what someone else is saying or doing. Rob's desire for immediate improvement in his listening habits caused him to lose focus. We had to remind Rob that it had taken him many years to develop his listening habits and that changes may not be obvious overnight. Keep in mind that the goals and techniques of self-monitoring are first to observe before changing a behavior or attitude. After self-monitoring you make a choice about one or more habits to improve, and finally create a step-by-step process toward goal achievement.

If these ideas don't make sense initially, don't force them into practice. Some good ideas may not work for you—and only you can make the call.

Tip #2: Avoid feeling like you must know everything about listening before taking steps to change.

The acronym ABD stands for "all but dissertation." We've seen dozens of graduate students fail to complete their dissertations (and, consequently their doctorates) because they refused to stop doing research and reading and, consequently, never wrote what they discovered.

Some of us fall into a similar trap of wanting to keep reading and thinking about listening ideas, rather than taking action. We simply can't learn everything about listening at once.

Rosa Ann, a hotshot MBA, had four management positions since she graduated from Wharton three years ago. At first she thought she was climbing the corporate ladder, but later realized that she was being shuffled around. After receiving her last performance review, Rosa Ann took the comments about her poor listening skills more seriously. Determined to succeed, she went to the Internet and searched for everything she could about listening. Within a month, she had read dozens of articles and three books about listening. When Rosa Ann's boss asked about her personal development plan, she told him what she had been doing to learn about listening. He was impressed with her research efforts, but asked, "Now that you've read everything you can, what are you going to do? Just reading isn't enough."

While learning about listening can lead to improvement, great strides are only possible when we are willing to put that knowledge into action.

Incentive

To change our listening habits, we must determine how important our desire is. If the desire is not strong, we have little incentive to improve.

> Mike, a software developer from Silicon Valley, sent his assistant, Phil, to one of our seminars in Santa Barbara. Phil had been told, during his performance review, that he needed to improve his listening skills at work. Phil's department had to do several costly and time-consuming reworks because of his listening mistakes. When Phil introduced himself at the seminar, he confessed that he didn't really want to be there—but would not get a raise unless he completed the workshop. His attitude during the workshop was one of indifference. All he wanted was the completion certificate so he could prove to his boss that he attended. We never heard from Phil again, but are willing to bet that his listening habits didn't change one iota after the seminar.

We have to ask ourselves hard questions. "Am I ready to sacrifice my old habits?" "Do I have a real desire to change?" If the answer to either of these questions is no, there is probably little reason to continue reading. If your answer is yes, you'll have a great chance to succeed.

Tip #3: Set up a reinforcement system for yourself. Reward yourself with a snack, a break, or even a shopping spree when you notice major success.

> Marilyn had been working on her bad habit of interrupting direct reports for two months. She used self-monitoring and had seen some progress. As part of her incentive plan, she committed to buy herself a new pair of earrings (as a reminder of listening) when she went through an entire week without interrupting her direct reports. When Marilyn made it through a whole week she went to Zales Jewelers and bought the earrings. She found a matching necklace that she planned to buy when she had gone through an entire month without falling back into her old habit.

Both tangible and intangible rewards can provide incentives. Decide what motivates you and work toward receiving your reward. Over time, your improved listening skills will provide you with countless rewards of their own.

Practice

Training and incentive provide the foundation for changing habits. Practice is the final step. Keep these two points in mind when practicing your new skills:

Tip #4: Set small, specific goals for yourself. If goals are too broad or vague you can get off track and lose sight of them.

Michelle, a college student at Tulane, realized that she had a lot of ineffective listening habits to work on since her friends often commented that they thought she wasn't listening. She listed those that she felt were most critical and prioritized her list. She decided that her eye contact needed the most work, so she made a plan to work on that single habit during the coming week. Although she was tempted to work on all five of her priorities at once, she realized that starting with a single habit gave her the best chance for success. After seeing true progress in improving her eye contact, she added her second priority—stopping daydreaming—after a couple of weeks. For Michelle, success came through setting specific attainable goals and taking them one at a time.

Set a goal, make sure it's attainable, and then start practicing!

Tip #5: Be persistent.

Persistence is more important than force. Philosopher J. G. Bennett emphasized this when he said, "Drops of water wear away a stone—but a cloudburst will leave it unchanged."

Margaret and Kale were good friends and played bridge every Tuesday at the country club. They had both completed one of our workshops in Omaha and made a pact to help each other improve. Margaret was action-oriented, and made specific plans to improve her listening in a variety of ways. She jumped in feet first and tried to become a better listener overnight. For a day or two she succeeded. But when she went on vacation with her family, Margaret forgot her goals and by the time she returned, she decided her efforts were in vain and just "gave up" trying. Kale, on the other hand, took a gentler and kinder approach and decided to work on just one habit initially, until she had changed it for the better. She was patient and persistent. Although Kale had several habits that still needed work, her persistence allowed her to show significant improvement and grow as a listener.

Accept that progress may be slow and that you may forget your goal at times. To slip back and fail temporarily is to be expected.

REFERENCES

1. (September 1998). The Husband Makeover. *Ladies' Home Journal*, 146.
2. S. Covey (1989). *The 7 Habits of Highly Effective People*. New York: Simon & Schuster.
3. W. Apple, L. Streeter, and R. Krauss (1979). Effects of pitch and speech rate on personal attributions. *Journal of Personality and Social Psychology*, 37, 715–727; T. H. Ostermeier (March 1990). Electronically-produced 'fast talkers' in TV/Radio commercials: What happens to the 'speeding listener'? Paper presented at the International Listening Association Convention, Indianapolis.
4. R. N. Bostrom and C. L. Bryant (1980). Factors in the retention of information presented orally: The role of short-term listening. *Western Journal of Speech Communication*, 44, 137–45.
5. Excessive Talking. (June 1998). ABC 20/20.
6. R. Greene, and J. Elffers (1998). *48 Laws of Power*. New York: Viking.
7. (1998). *Media Guide*. International Listening Association.

7

Listening Makes It Better:
Good Listeners Are
Always in Demand

In the 1980s, popular country singer Mickey Gilley recorded "Looking for Love"—a song that depicts misguided people who are "looking for love in all the wrong places" and "on all the wrong faces." We believe that something similar is happening with listening. The number of self-help groups, psychologists, psychiatrists, social workers, and cyber chat rooms continues to increase dramatically, and the number of divorces and crisis lines continue to soar. A common theme for these people reaching out personally or professionally is the need to talk and to have others listen. In fact, some hotels offer a new service to stressed-out or lonely travelers. For two dollars a minute, guests can call a licensed psychologist who listens to problems and provides a friendly ear.[1] These trends suggest that individuals of all ages are looking for people who will listen because there are not enough GOOD listeners to go around.

In John Grisham's book *The Street Lawyer*, the main character, Michael Brock, expresses his thoughts on homeless people:

I was rapidly learning that one of the challenges of being a street lawyer was to be able to listen. Many of my clients just wanted to talk to someone. All had been kicked and beaten down in some manner, and since free legal advice was available, why not unload on the lawyers?[2]

Like the homeless people Michael Brock encountered, many of us do not develop satisfying intimate relationships. In our transitory society, we often fail to build new relationships or make the time to really get to know each other. Superficial acquaintances rarely provide the involvement, understanding, and caring most of us desire.

New to the city and working in a virtual office as a computer programmer, Lisa rarely spoke with or ventured to the corporate office in downtown Manhattan. After spending nine hours a day in front of a monitor, she longed for human contact. Lisa called home frequently but did not want to admit her unhappiness or worry her parents. She did not express her feelings of loneliness and depression. Her parents rarely asked questions and focused on their own activities.

Fortunately one of Lisa's friends from high school, Nancy, noticed the sadness in her voice and asked, "Lisa, what's really going on? You were so excited about moving to New York, but now your voice sounds flat." Lisa attempted to make light of the situation by saying she was tired, but Nancy pressed on, "Come on, we've been friends for years. You have more energy than anyone I know . . ." After talking for another twenty minutes, Lisa finally opened up and expressed her feelings. Nancy did a great job of asking questions and repeating what she heard without giving advice. By the end of the conversation, Lisa had more energy in her voice. She expressed, " I can't believe how much better I feel. I just needed someone to listen to me."

Just as trained counselors learn how to care, demonstrate concern, and foster open communication, you too can develop more effective listening skills with the people you care about most—family members, friends, and co-workers. You can learn to create an environment of trust, to build rapport, and to encourage others to talk. Chapter 4 highlighted how irritating listening habits hurt the ones you care about most, while this chapter describes what you can do as a listener to strengthen your relationships and provide more meaningful feedback.

Characteristics of Effective Listeners

One of the most interesting exercises in our seminars begins by having participants identify a person whom they feel exemplifies the highest level of listening ability possible. We then ask them to list three or four characteristics the listener possesses. As participants go around the room describing their best listeners, often deep positive emotions surface. It's no chance event that people whom we regard as outstanding listeners are also people for whom we have deep affection. We then capture the characteristics on a flipchart and see how much overlap there is among characteristics shared by several outstanding listeners. The final part of this exercise is to ask participants to look at the list of characteristics and identify those that they feel they possess. They also identify some characteristics that they don't currently have but would like to. Not surprisingly, listeners often desire to develop traits associated with different listeners' preferences than their own. We record their answers and they become part of the participant's individual self-improvement plan. Some of the most frequently identified characteristics of effective listeners include:

patient

caring

loving

understanding

selfless

attentive

poised

generous

open-minded

thoughtful

intelligent

empathic

involved

As you can see, it is easy to identify characteristics we value in good listeners. These characteristics, along with other effective listening activities, have been evaluated in recent years.[3] In *Harvard Management Update*, for example, the author presented the following portrait of the manager with excellent listening skills:

> You're sitting there looking at the customer, asking probing questions and giving him or her more than enough time to answer. You're clearly communicating the importance of every word you hear by taking notes, leaning toward the speaker, and nodding to show you understand or agree. In other words, you're absorbing information like a sponge and doing everything but talk—to let the person know that's what you're doing.[4]

In every walk of life—not just in sales or management—this open, attentive, nonjudgmental style of listening helps communication, understanding, and relating.

The therapist asked her to describe what being in love would be like. After some thought, my friend said that if someone really, really listened to her, THAT would be her idea of being loved.
—Dear Abby (November 15, 1998), Universal Press Syndicate

Successful Strategies for Improving Listening in Relationships

As we discussed in Chapter 1, effective listening rewards you personally when you show others you care. While listening effectively also benefits us in our everyday interactions, there are occasions when it is particularly valuable:

- in the beginning of relationships
- when you don't understand another person's perspective/motivations
- when you and someone else have differing points of view
- when another person is angry or upset
- when giving or asking for feedback

Below are some tried and tested listening strategies that can help you improve your relationships at home and at work.

Know When to Be Silent and When to Speak

The biblical suggestion that "for everything there is a season" was echoed in the classic folk song "Turn, Turn, Turn." There is a season for speaking and another season for listening. Knowing when to listen and when to speak and being able to accept these different roles at the right time is a key to listening success.

"... If it won't distress you too much to talk about it, I'd like to hear about it."

It was the one time in his life that he ever approached a telling of the experience inclusive of its harshest, most painful particulars. What abetted his emotional control ... was the upholding, absolutely silent, mandarin-like way his father listened.

—Jeannette Haien, *Matters of Chance* (1997)

Pat craves action. She is an adrenaline junkie. For her, speaking is easy. She can carry a conversation on her own without even trying. However, it's very hard for her to keep her mouth shut and just listen without showing impatience through behaviors such as finger tapping, foot swinging, or playing with her car keys. She has been working to become more aware of how long she talks and interrupts others but confesses she still has a long way to go.

There is a silence that matches our best possibilities when we have learned to listen to others. We can master the art of being quiet in order to be able to hear clearly what others are saying ...

—Eugene Kennedy

The simple act of being quiet and listening is one of the most challenging for people who are extroverted, have high energy, or crave action.

To use the principle of silence effectively:

- pause a few seconds before responding
- accept silence as a normal part of conversations
- work to balance speaking and listening time during conversations
- break eye contact momentarily to allow others to feel comfortable with silence

Put a Lid on It: Keep Emotions Under Control

Emotions are wonderful until they take control of our mind and body.

Faith came from a family that expressed opinions openly and directly. Arguments often got loud and out of hand, especially at the dinner table. When Faith entered college and became Loretta's roommate, she felt no hesitation in criticizing Loretta's clothes, hairstyle, and even choice of boyfriend. When Jeannine, the dorm counselor, told Faith that Loretta had requested a change of roommates, it came as a shock. Faith really liked Loretta and thought they were good friends. After several counseling sessions, Faith realized how her blunt comments impacted Loretta, and she made a commitment to control them better in the future. However, Faith's habits were so deeply rooted that she still forgot herself at times and let her opinions spill out. Loretta returned to Jeannine in frustration. Jeannine persuaded Loretta to hold off changing roommates for a couple more weeks and to work on her own reactions to Faith rather than wait for Faith to change her blunt expressiveness. It was difficult at first, but soon Loretta was able to self-monitor her own reactions to Faith and let the criticism roll off her back. The two eventually stayed roommates and remain friends to this day.

Like Loretta, most of us have had our emotions take over when someone criticizes us or something we value. We may have reacted similarly and tried to avoid or escape the person and/or situation. Those of us who are more aggressive may have begun thinking of immediate comebacks or readied ourselves to engage in verbal warfare. Neither reaction is very effective in the long run. When emotions interfere with listening, they not only decrease understanding but also damage relationships. Here are a few tips to stop emotions from taking over and help "put a lid on it":

- be aware in advance of people and topics that trigger emotions
- analyze why you react to some words and ideas emotionally
- resist the temptation to get defensive
- empathize and remember that the speaker may have different meanings for words than you do
- withhold judgments until the speaker is finished

When you let someone else win an argument, often you both end up winners. If one of my children says, "You never spend any time with me," my impulse might be to respond, "But I spend lots of time with you. Don't you remember just yesterday we went out to lunch?" What I have found, however, is that my willing participation in an argument does nothing more than keep it alive by feeding it with attention.

Sometimes a better response is, "You're right. I hope we'll start spending more time together. I love you so much."

—Richard Carlson, *Don't Sweat the Small Stuff with Your Family*

Show Interest

The gift of focusing our attention on others is one of the greatest we can give.

> Rebecca's parents spoiled her as a child. They gave her a pony on her third birthday, and the gifts just kept on coming year after year. There were the diamond earrings at age ten, the ski boat at fourteen, the Corvette at seventeen, and a condo when she went to college. A lot of guys were attracted to Rebecca not only because of her money and good looks, but because she remained aloof and uninterested in their attempts to impress her. That was until she met Kevin. He didn't buy her expensive gifts or brag about his sports ability, investments, or career progress. What he did do was ask Rebecca questions and listen thoughtfully to her answers. His sincere interest broke through her defenses and let her real emotions surface. Kevin sensed the truth about her. Because her parents had showered her with material gifts all of her life, what she really craved down deep was someone to give her the gift of caring listening. That was five years ago, and now Rebecca and Kevin are trying hard not to spoil their own three-year-old daughter.

When everything else fails, listen! That's a lesson Kevin had learned early in life, and it paid off in building his relationship with Rebecca. In fact, according to one report studying 130 couples, the key to long-lasting marriages is a husband that listens to his wife and accepts her influence.[5]

■ Listen Across Time.

Another way to grow relationships is by showing interest in others across time. When we use what we have heard in subsequent conversations, we demonstrate we value people enough to remember wha they said. Salespeople are particularly adept at listening across time. Most maintain client files with notes for easy retrieval to use during their next sales call. Successful sales people know that maintaining a commitment to listening attentively over time strengthens relationships. Successful marriage partners have learned similar lessons.

> Cody thought the sun rose and set on Belinda. Their marriage of twenty-five years had seen them through thick and thin, happiness and sadness, and countless divorces by their friends. When asked at their silver anniversary party the secret of their relationship, they both gave the same answer: "We love each other enough to keep listening."

At the beginning of a relationship it's easy to remember to listen. There is still the thrill of the chase, and the excitement of a new relationship. Yet after we become more comfortable with our relationships we may fail to listen as carefully. What's hardest is to keep on listening through the tough, boring, and sad times. Those of us who remember to keep on listening seem to also be lucky at love!

■ Remember People's Names.

Another way to show interest is to remember a new acquaintance's name after you've been introduced and use it later in the conversation.

> David built bridges and skyscrapers for a living, was the president of a successful commercial construction firm and an active civic leader. Although he was accomplished as a contractor, he was even more successful as a fundraiser for

local charities. His secret weapon was his ability to make people feel like he really liked and cared about them on first meeting. David had trained himself to pay special attention to people's names and remember them after hearing them only once. When he greeted new acquaintances by name the next time they happened to meet, they were impressed and felt important. Relationships were developed and funds were raised thanks in part to David's special effort to re-member and use people's names.

Here are a few tips that can help you better remember names:

- repeat the name immediately after you hear it
- use the name within thirty seconds after you hear it
- associate the name with something or someone familiar
- collect business cards of the people you meet, and review them later
- write the names down as soon as possible after hearing them

■ Use Eye Contact Effectively.

Some say that inner emotions are revealed only through our eyes. As we've already discussed, eye contact is one of the primary keys in establishing and defining relationships. Through eye contact we also observe and analyze feedback, look for "turn-taking" cues that let us know when to enter conversations, show empathy and interest, and reveal our emotions. However, not all kinds of eye contact produce positive results.

Stanley had heard somewhere that eye contact was impor-tant to make friends and influence people. He took the ad-vice to heart and tried to hold eye contact long and hard in all of his face-to-face conversations. He found, however, that often people seemed to be uncomfortable when he held their gaze too long. He even had a hard time getting second dates after first dates when he literally stared at his partner all evening.

Stanley learned the hard way, that too much of a good thing, even eye contact, can be bad. Researchers have found that uninterrupted gaze (a stare) is not necessarily threatening, but usually indicates a "demand for a response, and in a situation where no appropriate response is apparent, tension will be evoked and the subject will be motivated to escape the situation."[6] The best eye contact between listeners and speakers is consistent but not constant. We need to make eye contact often enough to show speakers were are interested and concerned, but not so much that it makes them uncomfortable.

■ Make It Easy for Others to Talk

Most of us have been guilty of interrupting or discouraging others from talking. The listening technique of tracking encourages others to keep talking while you listen. Tracking is a term used to help others "keep on track" and keep talking. Some useful tracking behaviors include showing encouragement through head nods, keeping good eye contact, using silence constructively, and being sure not to interrupt. When we want to get another person to give us information or to uncover what the other person is thinking or feeling, tracking can help.

Cathi was a clinical researcher for a contract research organization in Connecticut. Daniel, her immediate supervisor, had called her into his office for a performance review. Daniel began the review by asking Cathi to evaluate her own performance in the past six months in light of her target goals. As she began her self-evaluation, there were several long, rather awkward pauses. Daniel patently waited for her to continue, giving her positive nods and good eye contact. Cathi relaxed after a while and began to get a clearer focus on the areas where she realized that she had not met her goals.

Daniel's effective tracking skills allowed Cathi to identify her own needs, which in turn made the review much more effective. Daniel's temptation to jump in and begin taking over the conversation when the pauses occurred was great, but he overcame it!

Keep in mind that when you need to listen to someone with a halting communication style, you may be tempted to jump in too soon. Allowing others the leeway to fumble a little while getting to the point may be frustrating but can help create better communication and closer relationships. Remember these suggestions when using tracking as a listening tool:

- avoid interrupting
- demonstrate patience
- remain objective
- show nonverbal encouragement through head nods and eye contact
- use prompting phrases (e.g., "Go ahead" and "And then?")

Use Paraphrasing and Reflecting Skills

Carl Rogers, the late eminent psychotherapist, was one of the first to embrace and teach the value of "empathic listening" in clinical settings.[7] He believed that repeating back to others what you heard them say (paraphrasing) and what you thought they were feeling (reflecting) would aid in self-acceptance and understanding. His concepts of "empathic" and "active" listening also are valuable in everyday interactions. You don't have to be a therapist to "give" these kinds of listening, or a patient to receive them. They are valuable tools in a variety of listening settings.

Read the following statements and think of a word or words to describe what the speaker is saying and what the speaker is feeling.

- "Spring break starts next week. I was really looking forward to having the twins back home from college, but they called last night to say they've decided to go to the beach with friends instead of coming home."

  Saying: _____

  Feeling: _____

- "Do you know Brent Calloway? He just earned a Ph.D. in physics and was the first person in his family to ever go to college. I was his high school counselor and helped him get a scholarship."

  Saying: _____

  Feeling: _____

- "If my wife keeps me up one more night with her snoring, I'm going to sleep in the garage. I'm so tired that it is hard to concentrate at work."

  Saying: _____

  Feeling: _____

- "I just found out that we're going to have a baby. We've been trying to have a child for three years and finally we're going to have good news to report at the next family reunion."

  Saying: _____

  Feeling: _____

For most of us it is easier to repeat the content of what others say than it is to describe what others are feeling. Yet in the statements above appropriate descriptions of the feelings would include disappointment, pride, frustration, and joy.

Paraphrasing reinforces that we retained the content of what the listener said while demonstrating that we paid attention. As listeners, we use paraphrasing when we clarify messages by saying, "So you're suggesting that we wait until next week to go to the mountains," or "You want me to come to the meeting at 9:30?" When we fail to test our understanding or to interact with the speaker we run the risk of misinterpreting or missing details of the message, and of losing the speaker's trust. By asking questions, restating, or summarizing what has been said we can make sure messages have been interpreted accurately.

Paraphrasing strategies include:

"God, Vix . . . listen to yourself! Not everything has to lead to a career. I'd rather have talent than a career."

"You mean a career based on your talent?"

"No . . . I mean just have the talent."

"But what would be the point?"

"Not everything has to have a point. Some things just are."

"That doesn't make any sense."

"Half of what I say doesn't make any sense to you."

"I'm listening. I'm trying to understand."

"No, you're not. You've already made up your mind."

"That's not fair."

"Maybe it's not . . . but that's what I'm hearing."

—Judy Blume, *Summer Sisters* (1998)

- summarizing key points in your own words
- repeating ideas or phrases you have heard to the talker
- asking for specific examples when given generalizations
- identifying words with multiple meanings
- analyzing and adapting to the speaker's point of view
- testing for understanding by using preview phrases (i.e., "If I understand you correctly . . . ," "Do you mean that . . . ?" "So you're suggesting that . . . ?")

Nora Roberts provides an excellent example of the power of both paraphrasing and reflecting in a section from her novel *Inner Harbor*. Phillip begins:

> ". . . since you're the good daughter, is there a bad daughter?"
>
> "My sister has always been difficult. Certainly she's been a disappointment to my parents. And the more disappointed they've become in her, the more they expect of me."
>
> "You're supposed to be perfect."
>
> "Exactly, and I can't be. Wanted to be, tried to be, couldn't be. Which of course, equaled failure. How could it be otherwise? she mused."[8]

When Phillip paraphrases correctly, she responds in affirmation and is encouraged by his understanding to continue sharing information. Continuing with the same passage from *Inner Harbor*, Phillip effectively uses digging by questioning to clarify her nonverbal messages and moves successfully from paraphrasing to reflecting.

> ". . . So what happened?" he asked when she only frowned.

"It's nothing, really. My mother is angry with me just now. If I give in and do what she wants . . . well, I can't. I just can't."

"So you feel guilty and sad and sorry."

"And I'm afraid that nothing will ever be the same between us again."

By accurately identifying and expressing what she was feeling, Phillip reflected the emotional content of what she was saying. Reflection of feelings encourages more in-depth conversation from others. When we pinpoint the emotional states of others, they feel more understood, and even come to understand themselves better.

It is much easier to repeat key words or phrases to check on informational content rather than dealing with feelings. With reflection you move the intimacy of a relationship from the surface and penetrate to the core of what the person is saying.

As a young girl, Lacy learned to notice the emotional states of others and to ask thoughtful questions. Within minutes, strangers felt like Lacy was a long-lost friend. Instead of talking about herself, Lacy had a knack of getting others to talk and share stories usually reserved for only the closest of friends. Afterwards, these acquaintances assumed they knew Lacy, too.

Identifying feelings in others can be frightening to all concerned. When others sense you know how they feel, they, in turn, usually feel a sense of relief. Reflecting strategies include:

- asking yourself what the speaker is feeling right now
- analyzing the speaker's point of view

- noticing inconsistencies in verbal and nonverbal messages
- describing the emotional states of the speaker (i.e., "You are feeling, . . . ," "I sense that you feel . . . ?" and "Am I correct in saying that you feel . . . ?")
- using a vocal tone and other nonverbal actions consistent with the behaviors of the other person

---

"The first duty of love is to listen."   —Paul Tillich

REFERENCES

1. S. Khan (May 18, 1999). Psychologist offers travelers a friendly ear. *USA Today*.
2. J. Grisham (1998). *The Street Lawyer*. New York: Island Books, 240.
3. M. Imhof (1998). What Makes a Good Listener? Listening Behavior in Instructional Settings. *Journal of the International Listening Association, 12*, 81–105.
4. D. Stauffer (July 1998). Yo, Listen Up: A Brief Hearing on the Most Neglected Communication Skill. *Harvard Management Update*, 10–11.
5. S. S. Cohen (April 1999). You talk. He listens. *McCalls*, 52–60; J. Gottman (1999). *Why Marriages Succeed or Fail . . . And How You Can Make Yours Last*. New York: Simon & Schuster.
6. L. A. Malandro, L. L. Barker, and D. A. Barker (1989). *Nonverbal Communications, 2nd Edition*. Englewood Cliffs, NJ: Prentice-Hall.
7. C. F. Rogers (1961). *On Becoming A Person*. Boston: Houghton Mifflin.
8. Nora Roberts (1998). *Inner Harbor*. New York: Penguin USA, 74.
9. Ibid.

8

She Hears . . . He Hears: How Men and Women Listen Differently

The reason you don't understand me, Edith, is because I'm talkin' to you in English and you're listening in dingbat!

—ARCHIE BUNKER, *ALL IN THE FAMILY*

Al and Linda, married for several years, had a comfortable home in south Florida. Al, a baseball scout, who lives and breathes his job, and Linda, a homemaker, who wants to make their relationship close and happy, have a problem. Al doesn't listen, and Linda takes it personally. To address their problem, the couple agreed to be videotaped over a period of weeks for an ABC *20/20* segment entitled "Talking to a Wall."

The segment opens with several brief vignettes that show Linda trying to get Al to listen while he tunes out and does not respond to her. Deborah Roberts, the correspondent featured on the segment, interviews the couple and asks Al to respond to the videotape. He was somewhat surprised to see his lack of responsiveness, but was not apologetic and did not make a commitment to change.

Kittie Watson, a listening expert and one of this book's authors, was asked to appear on the segment and evaluate the listening challenges the couple faced. Al and Linda then agreed to complete the Listener

Preference Profile (discussed in Chapters 2 and 3), and Kittie analyzed their results. As you might guess, their preferences were diametrically opposed. Al was totally action-oriented, whereas Linda was highly people-oriented. After their differences were discussed, the couple agreed to try to understand each other better and committed to improve their interpersonal communication.

The *20/20* segment didn't give viewers a classic happy ending; after several weeks, Al still tuned Linda out more than he listened and consequently Linda was still frustrated. To help explain their differences, a professional colleague, Dr. Richard Halley, was asked to discuss his research looking at gender differences in listening. His work and that of countless other behavioral scientists demonstrate that when it comes to listening, there are some consistent gender differences.

This chapter explores the differences in the ways men and women listen. It also provides some practical suggestions about how to overcome listening barriers between the sexes. It's important to remember that, although research may suggest specific trends, individual differences that may not follow the norm sometimes exist in men and women.

Women's Biggest Complaint About Men: "They never listen."

When asked, "What does your partner do that makes you the maddest?" in Shere Hite's study on women and love, 77 percent of the 4,500 female respondents said "He doesn't listen." And interestingly, 85 percent of the same respondents said the most wonderful quality of their friendships with other women is the ability to talk freely without being judged.[1] Hite's findings reinforce previous studies that suggest that the most happily married couples are ones who perceive themselves to be listened to and understood.[2]

Arlene entered the house holding back tears. Her husband, Skip, working on being a more responsive listener and noticing she was upset, asked, "Looks like you're on the verge of tears. Would you like to talk about what's going on?" His compassion was just what she needed. As she began to talk, she started to relax and felt closer to Skip than she had in months. But just as she finished telling Skip about the confrontation she had experienced at work, Skip fell back on his old pattern and said, "Arlene, this is what you need to do . . ."

One of the reasons that women may feel that men don't listen is that when men hear another person, particularly women, complain or express feelings of discontent, men often feel a need to fix the problem. Most women would much rather have both men and women listen attentively with empathy than to have them attempt to solve their dilemma.

Do Men and Women Really Listen Differently?

Whenever we present our listening workshops or convention addresses, inevitably one of the first questions we're asked is: "Do men and women really listen differently?" Our participants have experienced much confusion, frustration, and bafflement when communicating with the opposite sex. Some hope that we will validate their observations and identify which gender really is the better listener. Most of all, many of them desire a clear strategy to build better understanding and communication with each other.

Relaxing in the den after a busy week, Buford was reading the latest Tom Clancy novel and Cherry was watching her favorite video, *Funny Girl*. Even though their son had six friends sleeping overnight, they didn't anticipate many interruptions except to be asked for snacks. After a few minutes, Cherry heard a crash and looked over at Buford, who didn't move. Thinking he would have more of an impact than she, Cherry asked, "Honey, will you go check on the kids?" When Buford didn't look up, she raised her voice and said, "Buford, are you paying attention?" Finally, Cherry poked Buford saying, "How is it you can tune-out everything?"

When working to explain the distinctions between men and women, researchers often ask, "When there are differences, are they innate or learned?" While you may have already drawn your own conclusions, theorists claim that both men and women can demonstrate feminine and masculine listening behaviors. The term androgynous is applied to women and men who have the capacity to exhibit both feminine and masculine behaviors.* Although the literature on cognitive processing suggests that there are innate gender differences, most behavioral scientists believe gender differences in listening are more influenced by our cultural socialization than by a biological predisposition.[3]

Supporting the gender-role socialization approach, developmental scientists believe that we learn our listening behaviors one step at a time. If, for example, we were to compare newborns, infants, and toddlers up to eighteen months old, we'd see little or no gender differences in their hearing or listening responsiveness. By the age of two, however, researchers document differences associated with gender.[4]

---

*The terms sex and gender are occasionally used interchangeably in casual conversation. However, social scientists make specific distinctions between the two words. The term sex refers to biological characteristics of individuals, whereas gender refers to socially learned notions of masculinity and femininity.

Victoria and Stanley, enthusiastic, intelligent children, interrupted other children, each other, and their teacher Miss Presley during class. Each time Victoria interrupted without permission, Miss Presley walked to her desk and said, "Victoria, it isn't polite to interrupt others." On the other hand, when Stanley demonstrated the same behavior, Miss Presley ignored it and said, "Stanley, I know you have a lot to say, but others need a chance to share their ideas."

Unconsciously, Miss Presley was suggesting that certain listening behaviors are associated more with one gender than another. The gender socialization we experience as children and the stereotypes we use as adults influence how we listen.

Gender-based Listening Stereotypes

Men		Women	
• Logical	• Judgmental	• Emotional	• Powerless
• Forceful	• Self-centered	• Self-effacing	• Accomodating
• Confrontive	• Impatient	• Compliant	• Caring
• Directive	• Powerful	• Subjective	• Empathetic
• Focused	• Defensive	• Timid	• Other-centered
• Interrupting		• Non-interrupting	• Patient
• Dominating		• Submissive	• Responsive
• Inattentive		• Attentive	• Understanding

How Do Men and Women Listen?

As you read the following principles, keep in mind what we said earlier that exceptions to every rule exist. We've chosen to highlight the listening differences between men and women that are well documented. Identifying these differences will help you understand the challenges that both men and women face when they communicate with each other. Each can be looked at as an advantage or an oppor-tunity.

■ Men listen with half a brain.[5]

When considering the stereotypes listed previously, most of us associate effective listening with women more often than with men. Women tend to notice both verbal and nonverbal cues more frequently than men do. Surprisingly, a biological explanation exists. Brain research studying hemispheric processing discovered that when men listen they process language using the left hemisphere while women process language through both the right and left hemispheres.* In fact, baby girls have a larger connector between the right and left hemispheres that allows data to move easily between hemispheres. Since emotions are processed primarily in the right hemisphere, and language in the left, men may not be able to connect words to feelings as easily or effectively as women may.

Left Hemisphere	Right Hemisphere
• Rational lobe	• Intuitive lobe
• Processes information logically	• Processes information abstractly
• Concerned with:	• Concerned with:
speech	spatial and visual tasks
mathematical reasoning	musical tasks
analytical reasoning	gestalt tasks

---

*This research is accurate for right-handed males and females. Left-handed individuals have inconsistent brain-dominance and processing.

During one of our media interviews, we described how men and women process information differently. The reporter began to nod her head up and down and related the following.

> Now I understand myself better. Just last night, my husband and I attended a large cocktail party with over one hundred people present. Standing with a group of people, my husband engaged in a conversation with my boss. Even though they were talking about our latest ratings, I found myself getting distracted by other conversations and voices around me. My husband looked at me curiously when after a few minutes I said the party was too noisy and I wanted to leave. He seemed better able to focus on his conversation while I dropped in and out of several conversations simultaneously.

It appears that men are better able than women to tune-out distractions. Since women naturally use both hemispheres to process information, they are more easily distracted by competing messages than men, who can focus on one message at a time.[6] To test this assumption, the staff of ABC's *20/20* replicated a study that instructed subjects to listen to one of two messages that were being presented simultaneously. The original study quizzed listeners about the content of the assigned message and found the males consistently performed better than the females. The women were more distracted by the competing message while the men were able to tune it out. Likewise, in social situations, women frequently attend to both what they see and hear, while men remember primarily what they hear.

■ Women are listened to less carefully than men.[7]

Numerous studies have assessed the effectiveness of men and women speakers and presenters. Consistently the results suggest that listeners remember more information when they listen to male speakers. In addition, both men and women report that they would prefer to listen to male rather than female speakers.

> Eliza planned to be the first woman in her class to become CEO of a Fortune 100 company. With both business and law degrees, she had the credentials, experience, and motivation to succeed.
>
> Eliza, however, was infuriated after her first senior-level team meeting. Fully prepared, she offered a suggestion about how to increase sales in the European market. The team of eight men and two women acknowledged her suggestion and moved on to other agenda items. Less than thirty minutes later, a male colleague, Mickey, proposed the same suggestion as Eliza and everyone loved it. No one acknowledged her input and all the credit went to Mickey for the idea.

Similar situations are reported to us on a regular basis. You may wonder why. Some of the differences can be attributed to women using softer and/or higher-pitched voices and less direct communication (e.g., "Don't you think?"; "You may not agree, but . . ."; or "I know this may sound crazy . . ."). Others are a function of cultural stereotypes about men being more powerful than women. Fortunately, with awareness and effort these obstacles can be overcome.

■ Men comprehend the gist of a conversation rather than exact words.[8]

While women tend to recall precise words and phrases after a conversation, unless the situation calls for it men retain only general ideas. Men seem to hear the facts during conversations and lectures without paying close attention to other details. This is in part related to differences in how men and women process information through dominant brain hemispheres. Consider the following conversations:

What Gustav would relate to his wife:

"I saw your mother today."

"Where did you see her?"

"At the grocery store."

"Oh, really. What did she say?"

"Not much, just asked when we were coming over and something about stocking up for the holiday weekend."

What Gertrude would relate to her husband:

"I saw your mother at the grocery store today. She was shopping to beat the holiday rush and wanted to make sure she bought the grandchildren's favorite foods. She reminded me to prepare my special chocolate decadence dessert. She also asked what time we were coming over. She reminded me she's cooking a standing rib roast and doesn't want it to cook as long as it did the last time we had a family gathering."

"What did you tell her?"

"I said, we'd have to call her because Jermaine is working Saturday afternoon, Lovelace has band practice, and you've got an appointment with a client."

■ Women ask more questions than men do.

As we discussed in Chapter 3, there are more women with a people-oriented preference than any of the other listener preference types. Women use questions to initiate and maintain conversations. When women direct a series of questions at others, they're usually searching for ways to connect with them. Unfortunately, men may feel that women who ask a series of questions are checking up on them rather than showing care and concern. In fact, in one study where couples were instructed to maintain a conversation with each other, the women asked five times as many questions as men.[9]

> Newly married, Phyllis wanted to show her husband how much she was interested in his work. Each day when she heard her husband's car in the drive, she started thinking of questions she wanted to ask Peyton about his day. As soon as he entered the kitchen, she asked about his drive home, the number of sales he made, what appointments he'd scheduled for the next day, and if he'd gotten a chance to make reservations at their favorite restaurant for dinner. Peyton felt bombarded and overwhelmed by Phyllis's questions. After only a month of marriage, he found himself dreading his new wife's nightly ritual. He began to think that she lacked confidence in him and decided to ask her why she asked so many questions.

While showing interest in others helps to build and maintain relationships, you can see that it is wise to consider your purpose, frequency, and timing before asking a series of questions.

■ **Men in the therapeutic professions can be as skilled as women at interpreting feelings.**[10]

Some of us tend to accept the idea that men are insensitive and women are sensitive rather than looking at each person and situation individually. While research studies, popular books, and personal experience suggest that women of all ages interpret emotional states more accurately than men, men can learn to improve their effectiveness. Women tend to notice mood changes immediately, while men may take longer or even fail to identify subtle verbal and nonverbal cues. Professions that require nurturing, expressiveness, and artistic skills, however, train men to pay attention to nonverbal messages just as effectively or better than women. In addition to nursing, many male professionals in careers such as psychiatry, social work, counseling, teaching, and pastoral care have developed excellent skills in identifying and interpreting emotions and feelings in others.

Power Versus Relationship Issues

Women listen for different reasons than do men and have different communication goals. According to Deborah Tannen, men talk to create or maintain power while women talk to build and nurture relational connections.[11] Similarly, men and women demonstrate different verbal and nonverbal listening behaviors: men usually listen in ways that help them keep their power and women usually listen to build their relationships. When goals between the sexes are different, we may feel that we are communicating at cross purposes.

Letty had prepared a candlelight dinner for Reg the first evening they moved into their new home. Although boxes were still piled high and most of the unpacking was ahead, she wanted to make the dinner romantic. When action-oriented Reg walked into the cluttered dining room, he frowned and immediately began talking about what needed to be done next. He even got up during the meal to look in an unmarked box to see what it contained. People-oriented Letty tried to steer the conversation toward more personal topics, such as how happy she was to finally be in a home that was truly their own. Reg either ignored or brushed off her attempts at intimate conversation. He continued working on their to-do list throughout the entire meal.

This example is stereotypical to be sure. However, it illustrates that men and women often appear to live on different planets (Venus and Mars?) when it comes to communication goals and objectives.[12]

Who's Better at Listening: Men or Women?

Women are generally given the edge as effective empathic and relational listeners, whereas men are perceived as better at focusing on content and evaluating inconsistencies in messages. Although it's tempting to make sweeping generalizations about the listening skills of both sexes, research indicates only a few specific areas in which one sex tends to excel over the other: accommodating others, handling distractions, and interrupting others.

■ **Accommodating.**

Women are usually better at demonstrating a willingness to accommodate others than are men. The perception, real or imagined, is that women are more likely to look for ways to avoid direct confrontation or conflict than are their male counterparts. In most Western cultures, women are usually viewed as more considerate, cooperative, helpful, sensitive, submissive, and sympathetic.[13]

> Alice worked long hours as a receptionist at a tree farm. She was the only female employee in the office and her colleagues valued her highly. When Nash, her boss, was having problems with his teenage son, she gave him a willing ear and let him talk out his frustrations. When Carlos, the chief horticulturist, had to have back surgery, Alice took up a col-

lection to send him magazines to read in the hospital. Alice was competent in her job but was not an outstanding organizer or fast typist. Her ability to nurture and offer support through empathic listening made the workers at the tree farm perceive Alice as a better performer than she really was.

Based on the example above, you can see that accommodating is often a valued characteristic of friends and colleagues. However, when a person tends to give in too frequently, he or she is perceived as lacking influence, credibility or power.

■ **Handling distractions.**

Boys learn to deal with information overload by listening more selectively and tuning out distractions. In fact, some theorists claim that little boys get so much attention in kindergarten and elementary school classrooms that they learn to screen out much of what they hear. It's also probable that since most elementary school teachers are women, boys may be conditioned to tune out female voices more easily than male voices. This may be the reason why women may not be listened to as carefully as men in male-dominated business settings.[14]

Rob, originally from the northeast, grew up in a fast-talking, quick-paced family, while his wife, Carole, was raised in a more relaxed, easy-going southern atmosphere. Rob recently discovered the consequences of his family's style of communication: fading in and out of conversations. Rob was working in the garage when Carole came in and started talking. Rob was concentrating on his project but made sounds as if he were listening. He smiled occasionally, nodded his head, and even made um, and uh, um sounds. After a few minutes, Carole said, "Great, I'm glad you understand." Then Rob looked up and said, "Understand what?" Frustrated, Carole stomped out of the room.

Who was at fault in this conversation? Most would agree that Rob was guilty of giving the impression he was listening. But let's look at Carole. If she had been more direct, acknowledged Rob's distraction or had given Rob more incentive to listen, he probably would have paid more attention.

> Colin and Tawanda both worked in small cubicles along with thirty other telemarketers. Sometimes the noise level got so loud that Mary Ann, the marketing supervisor, had to walk through the aisle and give the nonverbal "shhh" signal to quiet her employees. Colin often wondered why Mary Ann was concerned about the noise since it didn't bother him in the least. He was able to screen out background noise from the other telemarketers and focus his energy on listening to his potential customers. Tawanda, on the other hand, often became frustrated with Mary Ann for letting the noise build up so long before taking any action. When the noise became too loud, she often lost her train of thought and couldn't remember some of the important information her potential customers were sharing.

As we mentioned earlier, men are usually better able to ignore competing distractions, whereas women have more difficulty.

■ **Interrupting others during conversations.**
As early as age three, boys interrupt girls more frequently. This tendency doesn't appear to lessen as men grow older. For example, a comparison of male and female mediators indicate that men interrupted

their clients twice as often as did women.[15] The exception is women who have advanced academic degrees. In another study, highly educated women surpassed men in the number of interruptions they made during conversations.[16]

> Ellis and Marjorie were vying for a promotion. They both were senior engineers at an oil refinery in Sulphur, Texas. Ellis was an action-oriented listener and tended to interrupt the line workers when talking with them about technical problems. Some of them became frustrated and complained to Clive, the process manager for the refinery. Marjorie, on the other hand, listened more attentively and tended to let the workers give full explanations concerning production issues before asking probing questions. The workers gave Clive feedback that Marjorie was the more competent engineer. In this case Ellis's tendency to interrupt cost him the promotion.

Gender differences can create natural tendencies and dispositions that impact listening skills. Since listening behaviors are primarily learned through the socialization process, they can be relearned or unlearned with effort. The ideal is to make the most of the typical listening advantage associated with your sex and work to learn skills often associated with the opposite sex that may improve your listening ability.

"He says, she says—but neither acknowledges what the other one says."   —Michael P. Nichols, *The Lost Art of Listening*

Three Strategies for Improving Listening Between the Sexes

Since most listening behaviors are learned, it is possible for both men and women to acquire new skills. As we discussed in Chapter 6, listening habits can be changed or improved with proper *Training, Incentive,* and *Practice*. Use the following strategies to help improve the quality of listening and relationships between men and women.

1. **Don't buy into male and female stereotypes about listening.** Earlier in this chapter we identified several cultural stereotypes associated with men and women as listeners. Stereotypes can be useful in helping us make good guesses about how people will behave and respond, but many stereotypes are inaccurate and don't allow for individual differences or individual improvement. Some of the negative gender-related stereotypes about listening that we need to overcome include:

   • Men cannot describe feelings.
   • Women seldom act assertively.
   • Women want to please others.
   • Men's voices convey knowledge.
   • Women's voices are weak and emotional.
   • Men are incapable of intimate or nurturing relationships.
   • Men do not notice nonverbal cues.

2. **Learn to empathize and show empathy.** Both sexes have the capacity to empathize but we tend to assume it is easier for women. If you have been told you have trouble understanding other people's points of view or want to make sure you are open

to learning more about empathy, consider the following two equally important steps. The first step is to actually become more empathic by putting ourselves in others' shoes and thinking as others would. The second is to demonstrate empathy to others—one of the most important listening tools to improve relationships.

Since it's impossible to know exactly how others are thinking and feeling, we first need to respond to our partner's verbal and nonverbal messages. In demonstrating empathy to others, it is important to use a sincere tone of voice along with open nonverbal messages. Below are several phrases that can be used to begin empathic responses without assuming you really know how the speaker feels:

- Could it be that . . .
- Correct me if I'm wrong, but . . .
- Is it possible that . . .
- It appears that you . . .
- I get the impression that . . .
- It sounds like . . .

Once you are more confident that you have correctly understood your partner's ideas and feelings you can use the following phrases to begin empathic responses:

- I hear you saying . . .
- You're thinking that . . .
- From your point of view . . .
- You're feeling . . . because . . .
- So you're suggesting . . .
- So you figure that . . .

3. **Change ineffective listening behaviors associated with your sex.** Usually our first thought is to get others to understand our point of view and change their behavior. But, as we pointed out in Chapter 1, listeners have the power. That means you have to choose to listen differently and go against expected stereotypes or learned behaviors. Since we can't make others change, we have to decide to change ineffective listening behaviors ourselves. The following lists provide the most common behaviors for men and women to avoid.

Men should:
- Avoid interrupting others
- Remember that women tend to send unspoken meanings behind words
- Work on understanding and interpreting feelings in conversations
- Try not to provide immediate solutions when women are upset or complaining; listen first
- Use "we" or "us" rather than "I" or "me"
- Adapt to *people-oriented* listening preferences if different than your own

Women should:
- Be willing to be more assertive
- Reduce the number of questions they ask initially when their significant other comes home
- Be patient when men tend to interrupt too much
- Avoid reading too much emotional meaning into men's verbal and nonverbal messages
- Refrain from becoming overly impressed or intimidated by men's voices and volume

- Adapt to *action*, *content*, and *time-oriented* listening preferences if different than your own.

> "Men build towers and women build webs."
>
> —Carol Gilligan, *In a Different Voice*

REFERENCES

1. S. Hite (1987). *Women and Love*. New York: Alfred A. Knopf.
2. L. Navaran (1967). Communication and adjustment in marriage. *Family Process*, 6, 173–84.
3. R. Boise, C. P. Hanley, D. Fansler, P. Shaughnessy, and D. C. Dudek (1984). Generality of observational skill across verbal and nonverbal modes: Literature review and experimental test. *Journal of Nonverbal Behavior*, 8, 172–86.
4. A. D. Wolvin, C. G. Coakley, and K. K. Halone (1995). A preliminary look at listening development across the lifespan. *International Journal of Listening*, 9, 62–83.
5. J. Wonder and P. Donovan (1984). *Whole-brain Thinking: Working from Both Sides of the Brain to Achieve Peak Job Performance*. New York: William Morrow. M. Bryden (1980). Sex differences in brain organization: Different brains or different strategies? *The Behavioral and Brain Sciences*, 3, 230–31.
6. R. D. Halley (1975). Distractibility of males and females in competing aural message situation: A research note. *Human Communication Research*, 2, 79–82.
7. P. Mindell (1995). *A Woman's Guide to the Language of Success*. Paramus, NJ: Prentice-Hall; D. Tannen (1994) *Talking from 9 to 5*. New York: William Morrow and Company.

8. J. Gray (1994). *What Your Mother Couldn't Tell You and Your Father Didn't Know*. New York: Harper Collins.

9. S. Metts (1984). A reinterpretation of conversational dominance. Paper presented at the meeting of the Speech Communication Association, Chicago.

10. R. Rosenthal D. Archer, M. DiMatteo, R. Koivumaki, J. Hall, and P. L. Rogers (1974). Body talk and tone of voice: The language without words. *Psychology Today*, 8, 64–68.

11. D. Tannen (1990). *You Just Don't Understand: Women and Men in Conversation*. New York: William Morrow.

12. J. Gray (1992). *Men Are from Venus, Women Are from Mars*. New York: Harper Collins.

13. C. L. Berryman and J. R. Wilcox (1980). Attitudes toward male and female speech: Experiments on the effects of sex-typical language. *Western Journal of Speech Communication*, 44, 50–59; L. Sholoff and M. Yudkin (1993). *He and She Talk*. New York: Plume.

14. M. Booth-Butterfield (1984). She hears . . . he hears: What they hear and why. *Personnel Journal*, 36–42.

15. C. Arnold and A. Clark (1996). Assessing listening behaviors of mediators in low and high coorientational accuracy settings. *International Journal of Listening*, 10, 65–87.

16. C. W. Kennedy and C. T. Camden (1983). A new look at interruptions. *Western Journal of Speech Communication*, 47, 45–58; L. R. Smeltzer and K. W. Watson (1984). Listening: An empirical comparison of discussion length and level of incentive. *Central States Speech Journal*, 35, 166–70.

9

Across Generations: Listening to Children, Teens, and the Elderly

If people would only hold their tongues on un-
pleasant topics, how the things themselves
would improve.   —E. F. BENSON

Listening to Young Children

Children have special listening needs, whether we are their parents, relatives, or acquaintances. Their language skills are developing by leaps and bounds, and their motivation to learn is high. They have more that they want to say than they have the words or capacity to express. They also want and need more attention when trying to communicate with adults.

> Mike wanted to ask his first-grade teacher, Miss Kirby, a question. Sitting at another child's desk, Miss Kirby didn't see Mike raise his hand or hear him say her name. When she didn't respond, Mike walked up to her, took her face in his hands, and turned her face toward him, and asked his question.

143

What Mike was asking for in this example, was "whole-face listening." A key principle when communicating with young children is to give them your full attention and whole-face listening whenever possible. We have to remember to show children with our face and eyes that we are paying attention.

It's also important to be the best listening model possible around young people. Whether we like it or not, we become listening models to all children with whom we come into contact. If they are our own children or kids we see often, then our modeling impacts them more than we might imagine. Keep in mind that the listener preferences children observe in their parents and teachers influence their own preferences as they mature.

ROSE IS ROSE ® by Pat Brady

Elias, a single Dad, is sitting on the floor in the den with his five-year-old son Robin. Robin is watching an episode of the Teletubbies on TV that focuses on a bully at the playground. Elias is reading the newspaper. Robin is restless and distracted. He loses interest in the TV show and scoots toward his father. Robin taps his father's leg to get his attention and says: "Daddy, I don't like Marjorie."

Elias sets his newspaper aside, puts the TV on mute, and looks at his son with caring eyes and asks: "Did something happen to make you dislike her?" Robin looks down and seems a bit frustrated and embarrassed. Elias adds: "It's okay, you don't have to talk about her if you don't want to."

Robin looks as if he might cry and eventually says: "She told Miss Brown that I did a bad thing."

Elias maintains a pleasant noncritical facial expression. "Did Marjorie tell the truth or did she make up a story?"

Robin begins to cry. "Daddy, I didn't mean to hurt Ginger, but when she called me a bad name, I pushed her down and she got dirty."

Elias responds firmly but evenly: "I'm glad you told me about Ginger. We both know that pushing is not nice, and we'll talk more about it later. Next time, why don't you let me know as soon as you come home if you have problems on the playground? Okay?"

Robin nods tentatively, hugs his Daddy, and they continue watching the Teletubbies together.

We can use this example to highlight five specific listening tips when talking with young children. Elias used all five of them in his dialogue with Robin. They are:

1. **Keep eye contact with children when they are speaking.** Look at them with soft eyes to show caring when listening. Use "whole-face" listening as much as possible.
2. **Show patience when children are struggling to say something.** Their brains are bulging with new words and ideas, and it takes a little longer for them to put sentences and thoughts together. When emotions are involved, it may take even longer.
3. **Eliminate distractions whenever possible.** Put papers or reading material aside, turn the TV on mute, stop working on your computer, turn away from distractions and toward the child.

4. **Keep aware of the impact your feedback and responses may have.** Children are highly sensitive to your responses, including nonverbal messages. Your tone of voice, facial expression, frowns or smiles all color the way a child interprets your response.

5. **Ask questions to show interest and involvement.** Our questions show attention and concern. Keep them short and simple. Questions from adults also help children develop better listening skills.

Listening to Teenagers

If you are the parent, relative, teacher, friend, or acquaintance of a teenager you are keenly aware of the difficulty in keeping communication channels open. As teenagers strive to be more independent, they tend to close off communications with authority figures, especially parents. The strategies we use with young children are not always successful with teenagers. In fact, asking questions and keeping eye contact with teenagers may actually keep them from sharing their innermost feelings and ideas with you.

> Caroline and Manny knew that T.C., their fifteen-year-old son, showed signs of using drugs. T.C. had become withdrawn, kept his room locked all the time, had rage rock posters tacked on his walls, and hung around with a group of boys who had been in trouble with the police several times. Manny decided that he had to take action. He ordered T.C. to come out of his room to have a man-to-man talk. Manny had T.C. sit facing him across from his desk in his home office. When T.C. looked down and away, Manny ordered, "Look me in the eye, young man." Then Manny

fired off a series of questions and accusations that got no direct answers from the teenager. Before the interrogation was over, T.C. ran out of the room and out the front door. Manny cursed and felt completely frustrated. When he told Caroline about his failed attempt to communicate, she said that she would try again in the morning when she drove T.C. to high school.

The next morning T.C. was in his usual sullen mood when he got in the passenger side of the Toyota as his mother put the car in gear. Caroline opened the conversation by saying that she had heard T.C. and his father shouting yesterday, and wondered if T.C. was okay. Both T.C. and Caroline were looking straight ahead so there was no pressure on the teen to respond immediately. He mumbled something negative and Caroline did not respond. She merely reminded T.C. that she and his father loved him, and wanted to help if he had any problems or concerns. During the ten-minute drive, T.C. revealed no significant information about his drug use, but he did begin to talk about some of his other activities.

During the next week, the morning drive to school allowed Caroline and T.C. the chance to establish more open communication, and finally T.C. volunteered that he had some problems that he was not able to solve, and the drug issue came out.

A feature story in *USA Today* documented the effectiveness of car chats between parents and teenagers.[1] The author pointed out that car chats are especially helpful when discussing sensitive topics such as sex and drugs, because parents and teens can look straight head and not notice if the other is blushing. The article goes on to say that car time is important because parents have a captive audience and that there are fewer distractions. Like business meetings, car chats may need some warm-up time, like idle chitchat, before getting to more serious discussions.

Of course one of the best uses of car time is to just listen. When taking a group of teens in the car, parents can learn a lot about attitudes, activities, and concerns just by eavesdropping on their conversations. By tuning into conversations parents can stay in the loop and also get a good idea of which friends are best for the teen to hang out with.

Here are five additional tips to keep in mind when listening to teens:

1. **Don't ask too many questions.** If teens think you are prying or interrogating, they will shut down immediately.
2. **Be selective when criticizing.** Using a wrestling analogy, we recommend that you know when to go to the mat when criticizing behaviors and actions. Too many critical statements sound like nagging and lose their effectiveness.
3. **Reinforce attempts to share information.** Since keeping channels of communication open is the primary goal, making sure the teen is talking to you is essential. Reinforce teen-initiated conversations, especially ones that might involve negative or sensitive information.
4. **Be available to listen when your teen wants to talk.** Timing is everything. If it's important for a teen to talk, then that's the time to move heaven and earth and make the time to listen. Saying "Not now" or "I'll be available later" will communicate that you don't understand how important their issues are.
5. **Find environments where open communication is easier.** The car, as we already discussed, is often a great communication environment. Side by side on the beach, park bench, a rock, or by

a swimming pool can be great environments for communicating with teens. Sitting across from a teenager at a kitchen table or the desk in your home office is not as conducive to open information exchange as sitting side by side or at an angle.

Listening to the Elderly

Cissy sat at her mother's dining room table frightened and in tears. The comfort of her childhood home seemed in the distant past. What was happening to her mother? Why was she responding so defensively? Why was she talking about a job she retired from fifteen years earlier?

It took Cissy several months to realize that her mother was in the beginning stages of Alzheimer's disease. At first she tried to correct her mother's confused messages and hallucinations. These attempts resulted in increasing her mother's agitation and hostility. Now she realizes the value of listening differently. Instead of correcting her mother, Cissy plays along with her mother's fantasies. Once when she came into the room, for example, her mother told her the windows were open and birds were flying around her room. Instead of saying, "Mother, there are no birds in your room and the windows are closed" she pretended to shoo the birds out of the window and pull the window down.

Even though listening to Alzheimer's patients can be challenging, listening effectively to most elderly persons is not. Unfortunately, our society, and the media in particular, have painted a stereotypical picture of the elderly as hard of hearing, senile, confused, and mentally slow.[2] Therefore many of us feel especially awkward when visiting an elderly person in a nursing home, day care center, or residence. Even when an elderly person is hard of hearing, research reports suggest that he or she will pay more attention during the conversation.[3] Communicating with and listening to the elderly is not nearly as difficult as you may think.

Angel, the perfect son, at least according to his mother, called every afternoon after his father died just to check in. These conversations, while usually brief, were the highlight of her day and at least once a week she had a hard time saying good-bye. Since she was so afraid she would forget to tell him something, she carried a small notebook around in her housecoat pocket and jotted down things during the day. Even after saying she had covered everything, she'd often ask another question or share an incident about her finances, her grandchildren, the weather, or their next visit. Angel often said little, but stayed on the line, just listening. He was reminded how important it was for him to be patient, concerned, and attentive.

> You don't have to be responsible for someone's feelings to be aware of them and to acknowledge them.
> —M.P. Nichols, *The Lost Art of Listening*

None of us likes to feel rushed, but the elderly are especially sensitive to being treated abruptly and with disrespect. It is irritating and embarrassing to be yelled at, second-guessed, rushed, and talked down to. Many elderly people report feeling they are treated as if they are incompetent and/or like children.

Suggestions

Create the best listening environment by:
- speaking in a normal voice even when the person is wearing a hearing aid;
- avoid large social gatherings if the person uses a hearing aid; ambient noise often makes it difficult for the person to hear clearly;
- speaking at a normal rate and assuming the person will ask you to slow down if necessary;
- feeling free to hold the elderly person's hand to reinforce that you are listening;
- using eye contact to demonstrate your interest and involvement in what they are saying;
- listening attentively even if the story has been shared several times before.

The Gift of Empathy

When we work with hospitals, we are often asked, "Can you teach employees to be more empathic or is that just something people are born with?" Our answer is "yes" to both questions. Yes, we can help people learn how to use more empathic responses, and, yes, some people are born with an innate ability to empathize more than others.

The word empathy is often confused with sympathy. The Stephen Ministry developed by Kenneth Haugk focuses on Christian caregiving. Stephen ministers receive more than fifty hours of training and learn how to use empathic listening skills. This ministry makes a distinction between empathy and sympathy by painting a vivid picture.

Visualize an emotionally troubled person experiencing a life crisis in a ditch. A caregiver offering sympathy would get down in a ditch with the person and begin to feel his/her deep emotion. The caregiver would experience his/her pain. On the other hand, a person offering to help with empathy would stay on the ledge above the ditch. This caregiver would be in a better position to help the person in the ditch get out and overcome his/her emotional distress.[4]

> "It's nothing," she said sniffling.
> "Care to unbutton?" [Want to talk about it?]
> "I don't know why I tell you things."
> "I listen."
>
> —Dick Francis, *Longshot*

Robert Carkhuff has studied empathy in helping relationships for more than twenty-five years. His research has tested a series of scales to help determine how effective a person's helping responses are. These scales measure a person's empathy, warmth, and respect.[5] Responses to other people can be placed along a continuum from highly effective to highly ineffective. The goal of a helping interaction is to build trust, self-exploration, and understanding in the other person. An effective response has a minimum rating of Level 3. Using the following example, consider how responses might be evaluated according to the chart below:

Team Leader: "I'm happy to be assigned to this team. Some of you know me, but for those who don't, I'd like for us to schedule an off-site as a team-building start-up activity. I believe that we need to get to know each other before we can learn to trust each other and operate as a real team. One of my expectations is for us to work interdependently—we

Rating	Description	Response Example
Level 1	• Attacks or hurts people • Makes people wish they had not spoken	• "We already know each other and don't need any touchy/feely games to work together."
Level 3	• Responds accurately to surface feelings and content • Fails to provide a "value-added" response	• "You'd like for us to schedule a date for a team-building offsite and have us give a status report about our part of the project."
Level 6	• Notices both verbal and nonverbal messages • Helps person gain new insights and self-aware-ness • Identifies feelings and content that aren't readily expressed by people	• "You're really excited about being a part of this team and want to see it accomplish more than in the past. You're concerned that we'll rely on old patterns of communication if we don't clarify our roles and make concrete commitments about how we can best work together. You'd like to learn about who we are as people and our investment in the project by how we present our status reports."

need to keep others informed and include others impacted by our decisions. To get us started I'd like for us to hear a status report from each of you."

Showing empathy is an essential listening and communication skill that demonstrates genuine care, concern, and interest in others.

LISTEN UP

He knew the precise psychological moment when to say nothing.

—Oscar Wilde

REFERENCES

1. N. Hellmich (May 19, 1999). Car chats put families on the road to intimacy. *USA Today*, D-1.
2. C. G. Coakley, K. K. Halone, and A. D. Wolvin (1996). Perceptions of listening ability across the lifespan: Implications for understanding listening competence. *International Journal of Listening, 10,* 21–48.
3. W. A. Villaume and T. Reid (1989). An investigation of the relationships among listening ability, aging, and the use of aligning actions in conversation. Paper presented at the International Listening Association convention, Atlanta, GA.
4. K. C. Haugk (1984). *Christian Caregiving as a Way of Life*. Minneapolis: Augsburg Publishing House.
5. R. R. Carkhuff (1983). *The Art of Helping*. Amherst, MA: Human Resource Development Press.

10

Lend Me Your Ear: How Speakers Can Hold Interest and Attention

Most of our assumptions about why communication
breaks down are about the other guy. We take our own
input for granted.
—MICHAEL P. NICHOLS, *THE LOST ART OF LISTENING*

A few years ago, we overheard one side of a conversation while at an
airport pay phone.

> "Honey, I can't help it."
> "No, there was no other reason that I wanted to come to
> New Orleans."
> "I'm on my way home now and we can talk about it
> when I get back."

On the way back to the gate we noted the caller's frustration and
asked him if he were having a bad day. He said:

> "You wouldn't believe it. Last week my secretary was out so
> I arranged my own travel schedules. I flew down to New Or-
> leans this morning from Pittsburgh. After going to the
> client's office, I realized that I had arrived a week early. I

thought they wanted me here this week. When I called to tell my wife, she didn't believe me. Now she thinks I have other reasons for coming down here. . . . Now not only do I have an angry wife, but my boss is going to kill me!"

An old communication axiom states, "When messages are misunderstood, they will be misunderstood in just the ways that will do the most harm." Since listening is complex, we often don't realize how many ways we can miss what was heard.

Throughout this book we have looked at communication primarily through the perspective of the listener. We, of course, recognize that the listener role is only half of every communication. The issue of who should be responsible for communication effectiveness has been debated widely by communication scholars and practitioners. In our workshops, we show a clip from the movie *Ferris Bueller's Day Off*. The scene depicts two teachers talking in front of a class without observable concern for the students. The camera pans the room and shows students in various modes of disinterest, daydreams, sleep, and faking attention. As our participants laugh out loud, they express how much they can relate to these students. When we ask, "Who had primary responsibility for the success of communication?" most laypersons say that the speaker should bear primary responsibility. The more thoughtful respondents, however, acknowledge that listeners should bear at least half of the responsibility for the communication's success.

It is our belief that if both speakers and listeners would be willing to assume more than half of the responsibility for successful communication, the world would be a better place. Think about it. If each listener and each speaker agreed to take responsibility for at least 51 percent of the success of communication, breakdowns would be few and far between. Since each of us alternates between speaker and listener roles, we have the power in our own interactions to accept our share of the responsibility.

One way we can take more responsibility is by learning where breakdowns in listening are likely to occur. The following model of listening, the PIER Model, helps pinpoint where breakdowns occur and suggests ways we can head them off as speakers and listeners. When looking at the model from the listener's perspective, think about ways to actively get higher quality information from speakers. When looking at the model from the speaker's perspective, think about how you can help listeners better understand and value your information.

The PIER Listening Model

During our workshops we describe the complexity of listening using the PIER Listening Model—a progressive four-level process—*Perceiving, Interpreting, Evaluating,* and *Responding.*

PIER Listening Model

Speaker ← → Listener

Responding

Evaluating

Interpreting

Perceiving

As we communicate with others, we move through levels of PIER. When communication is successful, it forms a communication bridge; people understand and are understood. Unfortunately, when listening errors occur, accurate communication is all but impossible.

Perceiving: *Perceptions* color the way we listen

Hunter was sitting down for an evening of watching Monday Night Football when his daughter called. Instead of turning off the television and giving his undivided attention, he hit the mute button so he wouldn't miss any of the fourth-quarter plays. His daughter, Erika, was reminding him that his wife's fiftieth birthday was at the end of the month. She said, "Dad, I figured this all out. You can drive her over to my house for dinner. I'll get in touch with her closest friends and we'll surprise her. I'll prepare all the food. All you'll need to do is get the cake. How does that sound?" Snapping to attention when he heard his daughter's question, Hunter said, "I'll get the cake." The day of his wife's birthday, Hunter picked up the cake he ordered and waited for his daughter to come over with the food.

In this example, Hunter heard most of the message, but missed a vital detail. He was supposed to drive his wife to his daughter's house to celebrate her birthday. Since he didn't perceive all of the message, he failed to respond appropriately.

Perception requires using the senses. While we usually focus on hearing when we think of listening, hearing is only one of the senses required for effective listening. Sight and smell are also engaged as a part of the listening process. In fact, people who are deaf have learned to compensate for their disabilities by reading lips and smelling acutely and are subsequently some of the best listeners.

As in the case with Hunter in the example above, many listeners start out well intentioned with focused attention but soon find themselves getting distracted. When distracted, listeners unconsciously allow something to divert their attention and can miss vital information.

At other times, past experience may distort the way information is perceived. One of our friends, Jay, recently went with us on a saltwater fishing trip. Typically he fishes in freshwater lakes. So when the captain told him to cast between "bumps" on the ocean floor, Jay heard and questioned, "stumps on the ocean floor?" because that was what he found in lakes. Jay's past experience caused him to mishear the instruction. Had the captain not cleared up the misunderstanding, Jay would have spent long hours looking for stumps that would never appear in shallow water. Once he learned to sight ridges or bumps caused by wave action, he was successful in casting between them and catching some prize redfish.

Reducing Perceiving Errors

Listeners can help themselves perceive effectively by:	Speakers can help listeners perceive more effectively by:
1. Focusing attention and concentrating. • Commit to pay attention; commit not to be distracted by speaker's mannerisms (such as *uhs,* fidgeting, and nervousness).	1. Speaking a little more loudly than normal.
2. Removing or reducing distractions. • Close doors, close blinds, turn off the TV set so you aren't tempted to look out the window.	2. Removing or reducing distractions/interruptions.
3. Sitting or moving closer to the speaker. • Change seats, move chairs, stand closer.	3. Moving closer to the listener.

Interpreting: Most listening errors occur at the *interpreting* level

Kim, a manager who was born in Japan, and Nelson, who was born in the United States, worked for the same company. Usually they worked well together, but recently they experienced a difference of opinion about how to handle vacation and sick leave policies within their departments. Finally after a heated discussion, Nelson summarized and said, "So, Kim, are we finally working on parallel lines?" Slowly, Kim shook his head in agreement. During the next week, one of Nelson's employees complained that Kim's department had a more lenient sick leave policy. After asking for details, Nelson stormed into Kim's office and demanded, "Didn't we agree to work on parallel lines?" Kim looked puzzled, held up his hands to form parallel lines and said, "Parallel lines never meet." Nelson thought they had compromised, while Kim had agreed to disagree.

Whether or not perceptions are accurate, we try to make sense out of what we perceive. This is when errors are most likely to occur. A workshop participant related one serious consequence of an interpretation error.

A utility company was building a nuclear power plant in a rural community. Because local residents were concerned about the safety of nuclear reactors, the company's public relations department decided to offer tours of the new facility before any radioactive materials were brought on-site. The company placed announcements in the local newspaper as well as on radio stations. The first few days after the announcements went out, the department got dozens of calls to schedule tours. After the third day, however, the number of calls dropped dramatically, and by the fourth day no one in the community was calling. The public relations department discovered a rumor had started that the site was dangerous. In uncovering what happened, they discovered that on the second day a woman called to schedule a tour. At the end of the conversation, the receptionist said, "You will have to wear protective clothing." Before she could explain what she meant, the woman hung up. The fearful woman interpreted protective clothing as large yellow suits to block radioactive contamination. Had she waited to hear the rest of the message, she would have been told that the site was still officially under construction, and guests would have to wear hard-hats and hard-soled shoes as a safety precaution. This error cost the utility thousands of dollars in new ads as well as the loss of public trust and confidence.

Reducing Interpretation Errors

Listeners can help themselves interpret more effectively by:	Speakers can help listeners interpret more effectively by:
• Asking the speaker for examples —Examples help you understand complex ideas.	• Using relevant and specific examples
• Asking the speaker to clarify ideas or terms —Watch out for words that may have multiple meanings.	• Asking the listener to summarize or paraphrase.
• Repeating words or paraphrasing ideas and checking with the speaker —This will let the speaker know your level of understanding and allow for corrections, if necessary.	• Repeating major themes and summarizing.

Evaluating: *Evaluation* occurs before messages are complete

When do you first evaluate the importance of what you hear? Do you wait until the speaker stops talking, or do you begin to formulate the great comeback almost immediately? Our experience suggests that many listeners use their power to make up their minds about the value of information even before someone starts talking.

In the Academy Award–winning film *Broadcast News*, investigative reporter Albert Brooks asks William Hurt, a stylized news anchor, for advice on how to deliver on-air news. Before the coaching session begins, Brooks says, "I don't know how helpful this is going to be because we look at things so differently." Hurt replies, "We sure do." As the scene progresses, Hurt tells Brooks to look at the camera and to sit on his coat jacket to improve his visual appeal. Brooks ignores him and finally Hurt gets up and tucks the tail of his jacket under him. It was not until Brooks saw the results that he said, "Fantastic tip!"

In most cases, we first decide whether or not information is believable and then whether or not it is important. Most of us rush ahead of speakers and make hasty evaluations. One of the most dramatic examples is the space shuttle *Challenger* disaster. Engineers warned officials that the O-rings were defective and needed further inspection. Tragically, the information was judged as not critical enough to stop the launch. Only later did a full investigation discover the deaths of teacher Christa McCauliffe and the rest of the crew might have been avoided with a different evaluation.

Responding: The listening process is not complete until there is a *response*

Hank drops by a theater practice his best friend, Callie, is directing. He enters nonchalantly and receives an unexpectedly

Reducing Evaluation Errors

Listeners can help themselves evaluate more effectively by:	Speakers can help listeners evaluate more effectively by:
• Withholding judgment until the speaker is finished. —It's important to have all the critical information in order to make quality evaluations.	• Reinforcing critical points with energy verbally and visually.
• Asking the speaker about the importance of key points. —Do you and the speaker agree on the relative importance of the ideas?	• Helping listeners understand what's in the conversation for them.
• Asking the speaker about priorities for requested actions. —Which items are most important from the speaker's point of view?	• Emphasizing the importance of the message by using hard data (statistics, factual evidence, expert testimony).

cold reception. Callie reminds Hank that he missed the production he promised to attend. At that moment, a light bulb goes on and Hank begins apologizing for his oversight. Instead of asking why Hank failed to attend the play, Callie assumed he didn't value her enough to follow through on his commitments. In actuality, he forgot to write it down.

As in the case above, even an unintended response is a response. And the listener, Callie, has the power to decide how to interpret the message. She could have called to see why he failed to show or checked for understanding of the time, but as in this case she assumed Hank didn't value her friendship enough to attend.

This point is reinforced by a recent Dear Abby column:[1]

> *Dear Abby:*
>
> *Last Sunday was my wife's birthday, her first since our marriage in April. I didn't forget it, but the situation is as bad as if I had.*
>
> *About a month earlier, "Beverly" told me that she would like to spend her first birthday as my wife alone with me. She didn't want anything spectacular—just the day with me and maybe a nice dinner.*
>
> *Abby, it completely slipped my mind! I took the initiative and, being a thoughtful husband (I thought), made arrangements to take Beverly to her parents' house for the day. Well, her mood seemed to dim as the day wore on. When she finally told me what was bothering her, I felt terrible. She said I paid no attention to her request.*
>
> *I would love to take back that one day and start it all over the right way, but I can't. What can I do to make it better now?*
>
> *Guilty in Wilmington, DE*

The chance for a response error increases when the person listening is not responsible for acting on what was said. In fact, when we use another person to relay a message, we abdicate power and responsibility. One of our students reminded us of response errors at the drive-through windows of fast-food restaurants:

> I was asked to pick up sandwiches for my MBA study group. One member of the group, Tara, who hates mayonnaise, made it very clear. So, I placed the order and asked the cash-

ier to repeat my request. She repeated, "One grilled chicken sandwich without mayo; add mustard." When I got to school everyone opened their orders. Tara looked at me in disgust when she opened her sandwich and found a glob of mayo.

At fast-food restaurants and other business settings, more than one person often responds to a request. When there is an intermediary, communicators lose power and control of the outcomes because of lower-level errors, such as interpreting, which are often compounded as they travel from one person to the next.

Reducing Response Errors

Listeners can help themselves respond more effectively by:	Speakers can help listeners respond more effectively by:
• Taking notes and filing them carefully. —Note taking is the listener's most important tool for storing and retrieving information.	• Sending a written reminder.
• Avoiding jumping to conclusions too quickly. —Premature responses often cause hard feelings and breakdowns between listeners and speakers.	• Explaining positive and negative consequences of different listener responses/choices.
• Giving speakers immediate verbal feedback. —Feedback helps the speaker know you've been listening and helps avoid breakdowns.	• Asking listeners to identify actions they are going to take.

When breakdowns in communication do occur, the PIER Model helps diagnose where the listening error took place The move through the levels of listening is progressive, and all steps may take place in a fraction of a second. If we fail to perceive messages accurately, there is little or no chance we can progress to higher levels without breakdowns.

Some Reminders About
the PIER Listening Model

The Pier Model makes it clear that if you've seen one listening problem, you haven't seen them all. We can use the model to head off listening barriers before they become problems. Keep in mind the following points:

- Different kinds of problems occur at Perceiving, Interpreting, Evaluating, and Responding levels.
- What works best to avoid or overcome listening problems varies for each level.
- People with different listening preferences experience listening obstacles at different levels of the PIER process.
- Always try to identify and correct listening errors at the lowest level possible.
- Most errors occur at the interpretation level and go undetected until it's too late.

"I stop and taste my words before I let them pass my teeth."
—Anonymous

Considering the number of levels where listening errors can occur, it's easy to understand why communication breakdowns happen. In some ways, it's amazing that we communicate as well as we do on a daily basis. If our goal is to seek continuous improvement in our communication, then we need the best tools possible to be successful. The PIER model is one of the most powerful tools at our disposal as speakers and listeners to decrease listening breakdowns and improve the accuracy of communication.

REFERENCE

1. A. Van Buren (May 18, 1998). *Dear Abby*. Universal Press Syndicate, D, 1–2.

11

Winning by Listening Around: Giving and Receiving Feedback

I know you believe you understand what you think I said, but I am not sure you realize that what you heard is not what I meant.

—ANONYMOUS

The term feedback has taken on new meanings in recent years. Originally it referred to an acoustic response to an electronic signal. Now the term is widely used in business and industry as well as in communication courses and workshops. Feedback in an electronic circuit serves the function of closing the loop. Feedback in communication settings also refers to closing the loop. In this instance, the loop is between speakers and listeners.

One of the key roles listeners play is providing accurate and timely feedback. Unfortunately, many of us are not trained in how to give feedback clearly. Giving and receiving feedback is so critical in the business community that consultants and trainers make careers out of helping managers and executives learn to give and receive feedback effectively. The *Wall Street Journal* recently profiled an internal consultant for Damark Direct Sales Corporation, Mark Johansson, whose primary job is to help executives "look at people skills, leadership

169

skills, and how to improve."[1] Listening and feedback rank high on the list of skills Johansson considers critical.

In our work with managers and executives, we also have found a critical need for focused training in giving and receiving effective feedback. In addition, we have discovered a similar need among couples, parents, and friends.

Stefanovich, the company founder, was inspired to introduce Think Cards because his father, a Chevrolet executive, always carried around bits of paper filled with instructions and reminders. At Opus, they're a license to tell your colleagues—bosses included—what's on your mind. Perhaps someone is talking too loudly on the phone or playing favorites. "Think Cards are the ideal medium when you don't quite know how to say it," Stefanovich says. Signed or left anonymous, they're effective. Staffers frustrated with long meetings got them shortened. Employees unhappy with their cubicles are pushing for a redesign. And Stefanovich swears he's trying to talk more slowly.

Each of the 27 employees at the Richmond event management firm gets an unlimited supply of the red cards. Staffers drop them on desks, in pockets, or in a box at reception. "Anybody who's human will get one and say, 'Golly, I've messed up.'" Stefanovich says. "But one of our values is respect. Though the cards are candid, they are respectful."   —Carol L. Dannhauser, *Working Woman*[2]

Why We're Reluctant to Give Feedback

Lauren had been e-mailing with Ben for a couple of months. Their conversations at first were innocuous and chatty. Lately, however, they had become much more intimate and suggestive. Feeling drawn to Lauren, Ben asked if they could meet face-to-face. As soon as she got his message, Lauren called her best friend, Lizzie, and asked, "What should I do? You know that I have had an exclusive dating relationship with Victor for over a year. He doesn't even know that I've been on-line."

In this example, what does Lauren really want from Lizzie? If Lizzie acts as Lauren's conscience, then Lizzie can be praised or blamed for the consequences. Lizzie, like most of us, may be reluctant to offer feedback when she thinks that the person needs to take responsibility for his or her own decisions. While with children it may be important for parents to make some decisions, adults are usually accountable for their own actions.

At other times, we may not give feedback because we feel it is unnecessary. Some managers, for example, perceive semiannual employee feedback sessions as a time-consuming nuisance, especially when departmental functions are running smoothly. In addition, people who are more introverted may find it difficult to deliver feedback effectively, especially if it involves giving bad news. Even so, research reports suggest that employees feel they rarely get enough feedback about their performance even when the feedback is negative.[3]

Another reason some of us fail to give direct feedback is that we're afraid of what the other person's reaction might be. Telling a spouse that you think she would look better if she lost fifteen pounds, an employee that he is receiving an excessive number of personal phone calls, a customer that you lost her order, or a student that he didn't make the varsity baseball team is difficult. It is even more challenging when we anticipate the negative reactions a person may have to the feedback we give. We know that some of us withdraw, others get angry, pout, cry, or lash back verbally. Giving feedback effectively takes courage as well as practice.

How to Give and Receive Feedback

Without preparation and experience, most of us feel awkward giving feedback initially. The following suggestions should increase the likelihood that your feedback will be heard and help you make it with ease.

■ **Take time to prepare.**

Planning helps control distractions that may hinder another person's ability to listen.

> Timothy, a manager of service center representatives, works in an open office environment. With no walls or doors to obstruct sounds, all employees tend to overhear what others are saying. Conscious of the importance of giving confidential performance feedback, he looked for an alternative environment. Now he takes employees for a ride in his pickup truck when he wants privacy.

Ineffective listeners may not consider the need for privacy or modifying their environment. Effective listeners, on the other hand, prepare to maximize listening success and prepare to give feedback by:

- modifying the environment when necessary by finding a quiet place to listen, holding calls, shutting doors, or turning off televisions;
- collecting necessary materials before meetings when possible;

- putting distracting objects such as papers or rubber bands out of reach;
- removing barriers by moving out from behind a newspaper or desk.

■ **Focus on one behavior at a time.**

Brewer accepted a job as an assistant golf pro at the local country club. His first assignment was working with a group of five young professional women who had never picked up golf clubs. Confident since he was a scratch golfer himself, Brewer distributed long irons to the women and gave a few brief instructions. Then he asked each woman to take a swing and offered the following feedback:

"Okay, use an interlocking grip, bend your knees, keep your heads down with your eyes on the ball, pull away from the ball with your left hands and make sure your left elbows are in locked positions as you swing through to the balls."

While eager to learn, the women were overwhelmed with so many different messages. In frustration, one blurted out, "Stop it! I can't remember to do so many things at one time! Can't we start with one thing at a time? By the way what is an interlocking grip?"

Obviously with the example above feedback can be discouraging. To increase the odds of having others listen to and apply the feedback you send, focus on one behavior at a time. Rather than giving a laundry list of information, focus on what is most important, especially with improvement feedback. Once a person has absorbed and applied that feedback, consider giving additional information.

■ **Be specific.**

You may be saying to yourself, "I'm not the type of person who withholds feedback, in fact, I give it to others all the time." While we applaud those of you who give feedback regularly, we have found that most of it is general rather than specific. Consider the following:

Role	General Feedback	Specific Feedback
Parent	"Good job!"	"You've done a good job making up your bed, hanging up your clothes, and straightening your room. I feel encouraged that you're learning to take care of yourself."
Boss	"I'll do it myself!"	"When you miss deadlines, I think you didn't pay attention to my request and I lose confidence in your ability to follow-through with your assignments."
Teacher	"C+"	"C+. To improve your grade on your next paper, you need to: • structure your paper more carefully by including an introduction, thesis statement and conclusion; • cite at least four sources; • proofread and check for spelling errors."
Co-worker	"Thanks."	"Thank you for offering to help me prepare the brochures for mailing. I felt overloaded and appreciated your assistance."
Spouse:	"It doesn't matter."	"I like both restaurants and we haven't eaten at either of them for a long time. You decide."

■ **Give feedback regularly and consistently.**

Not long ago, one of our workshop participants said, "My wife knows I love her, I come home every afternoon, don't I?" For some spouses this might be enough to let them know that they are loved and appreciated. Yet most of us want and need more explicit, regular acknowledgment of how we are doing and/or how others are feeling.

> Dr. Cribble, a college professor at NYU, got negative evaluations from his students about his basic composition class. When the department chair investigated what prompted the negative comments, she discovered that he failed to return grades for two papers he had assigned until the last day of class. Students were frustrated because they didn't know how they were performing going into the final exam.

In this example the feedback at the end of the term was too late to help the students. Because this type of feedback in college classes is common, many universities are adding midterm course evaluations to the assessment process. Interim feedback can be used to modify the course or instructional design during the second half of the semester.

■ **Time feedback appropriately.**

> Lilleth, a guidance counselor at a middle school in Scottsdale, was the chair of the teachers' grievance committee for her district. She had the distasteful task of giving teachers and administrators negative feedback about their performance as part of her committee responsibility. She learned the hard way that timing of feedback is critical. She scheduled her first session after classes on a Wednesday afternoon in September. As it turned out, the teacher to whom she was to give feedback about his chronic late arrival at meet-

ings was, among other things, the junior high football coach. The coach's players were waiting outside the teacher's conference room for the coach to come to practice when he went into the feedback session. The coach was defensive to begin with about the accusations, and the time pressure to round up his players was just too much. He shouted at Lilleth when she gave him the committee's findings, and left the interview in a huff. Though he later apologized, Lilleth realized that her timing was off and scheduled follow-up appointments at more appropriate and less stressful times.

We've all received feedback that was inconvenient, embarrassing, or at a time when we had little energy left to listen. Use these guidelines when timing your feedback:

- Be sensitive to your own and the other person's energy level
- Select an environment that is quiet and comfortable
- Deliver the feedback as succinctly as possible
- Give feedback over several sessions, if there is a lot to give

■ **Learn from negative criticism and feedback.**
Our last suggestion focuses on our receiving feedback rather than giving it. Giving effective feedback is tough. Receiving it in order to learn and grow is even tougher!

Giuseppe worked on the docks in Boston Harbor. Millard, his foreman, asked to meet with him after work to discuss something important. Giuseppe told his fellow workers about the request and they all began to give him well-meaning advice. One told him to: "Shut up and don't say anything." Another told him, "Don't take any crap." Still another told him, "When the foreman called Jennie in last month, he gave her walking papers."

By the time the meeting with Millard began, Giuseppe was truly worked up. He listened with half an ear when Millard told him about a new process that was starting and that Giuseppe would need to take some additional training in order to keep his present job. Giuseppe missed the point and viewed the training as a threat to his job security. He reacted badly in the meeting and eventually was fired.

Had Giuseppe been able to view the meeting with Millard as constructive feedback, he would still be working on the docks. Like Giuseppe, many of us aren't mentally and emotionally prepared to learn from feedback we view as criticism. Here are a few ideas that can help us learn from negative feedback:

- Take a deep breath if you begin feeling tense
- Don't think bad thoughts about the person giving the feedback
- Separate the content of the feedback from the person who's giving it
- Think about how to avoid making the same mistakes later

Take the Static Out of Feedback Responses

One of the most irritating experiences we encounter when giving keynote speeches and public presentations is microphone feedback. The shrill squeal causes audience members to cover their ears, make faces, and/or recoil from the sound. Something similar occurs when we make unintentional comments that hurt, frustrate, anger, confuse, or embarrass someone else. The person often assumes a defensive posture and recoils from you and your message. Most of us are surprised when these unsuspecting comments create static in our relationships with spouses, children, colleagues, and friends.

As chair of her academic department, Irene was expected to solicit faculty opinions, suggestions, and input before sending departmental reports to the administration. Lately, most faculty members had not been responding to requests and were apathetic about meeting attendance. When the professors she considered her friends let her down, she called one of them at home.

"Jacob, this is Irene, I wondered if you have a few minutes for us to talk. There are several things I'd like to talk about."

"Sure, no problem, let me take the phone in the other room." When Jacob came back on the line, Irene began. "I've been wanting to talk with you for the last few weeks but have been reluctant because of our friendship. When you fail to respond to my departmental requests, miss our meetings, and put off observing the new faculty member's classes, I feel frustrated because we need your input to make the best decisions for the department. . . ."

Up to this point Jacob was agreeing with Irene and feeling regret for his behavior during the last few months. He said he was sorry. Feeling good about how the conversation was going, Irene continued, "I consider you my friend and I've done things for you I don't do for anyone else. I even asked the dean to give you a raise and put in your request for a new computer for next year and now you're letting me down." At this point, Jacob bristled and got defensive. Irene didn't realize that she had just hit a nerve. It was one thing to point out specific behaviors that frustrated Irene, but to imply that he didn't deserve a raise or an Internet-compatible computer was another issue.

Irene was confused by Jacob's defensiveness. She thought she was showing her support for Jacob, but he read her response very differently. What could she have done differently to avoid the negative reaction?

It is sometimes difficult to know how others will interpret our words, and there are many occasions and situations we find awkward. There are a number of self-help books that give advice on what to say in various business and social encounters.[4] Have you ever said, "I wish I hadn't said that" after a blind date or a job interview? Often the most challenging times to know how to respond appropriately are during emotional life transitions and crises when there is a death in a family, a marriage dissolves, someone loses a job, or a friend is diagnosed with a life-threatening illness.

During times of emotional stress it is best to avoid using pat or automatic responses. Consider the *dangers* associated with the following:

- I know how you feel.
- It will feel better in a few weeks.
- It's all in God's hands.
- You shouldn't feel that way.
- You're lucky it didn't happen last year.
- Let me tell you what happened to me.

■ **Instead, effective listeners can:**
- Ask how the person feels and then attend to their response.
- Notice inconsistent verbal and nonverbal messages.
- Answer questions honestly and directly.
- Use effective attending behaviors.

179

- Patiently listen to stories you've heard for the first or hundredth time.

> When I ran for governor, nobody thought I could win. But I never tried to hide who I am, in conversations, speeches, whatever, and people came out and voted in record numbers. But I also think listening is as important as talking. It's interesting: If you're a good listener, people often compliment you for being a good conversationalist. —Jesse Ventura, Governor of Minnesota
> (former professional wrestler)

Three Feedback Strategies to Manage Others

As we asserted earlier, listeners, even without conscious effort, tend to control communication outcomes. Understanding and using feedback strategically allows motivated listeners to manage their time and interactions with others. When practiced effectively, these techniques give you more control while maintaining ongoing relationships. These three techniques—*dampening, redirecting,* and *blocking*—will help you learn how to use feedback to manage others.

Dampening. Those of us who have taken piano lessons remember our teachers explaining the function of the dampening pedal. The pedal, when depressed, keeps the piano strings from continuing to vibrate. In effect, it stops the sound waves from continuing to flow and quiets the sound dramatically. Those of us without piano backgrounds have undoubtedly heard the expression that someone is a wet blanket, indicating that someone is not much fun or is too straightlaced to enjoy some excitement.

The concept of dampening can also be an effective feedback tool.

When we, as listeners, are involved in conversations or debates with others who are highly emotional, excessively vocal, or just plain excited, we can use dampening techniques to help calm them down.

> Denise ran home as fast as she could clutching her report card in her hand. "Mommy, Mommy, guess what, can you guess? Huh, can you?" She continued talking so rapidly that her mother, Stella, could barely understand what she was saying. Instead of interrupting her seven-year-old and asking her to slow down, Stella let her daughter run out of verbal and emotional steam before responding. She looked at Denise with an understanding facial expression, nodded to show interest and empathy, and just let her daughter rattle on. Eventually Denise ran out of breath, and at that point, Stella responded to her daughter's questions.

In this example, dampening involved saying nothing, and simply using nonverbal expressions to let Denise know she was being heard and understood. Dampening, however, is most often used when there are some negative overtones such as fear, anxiety, anger, or rage associated with the speaker's message. Here are a few suggestions for trying to calm or dampen emotions in a speaker:

- Avoid interrupting others until they have finished a complete thought or series of ideas
- Use your facial expressions and gestures to demonstrate understanding and empathy
- Use encouraging nods and remarks to help the person talk it out
- Don't take on or mirror the speaker's negative tone of voice or facial expression

Redirecting. Redirecting is a feedback tool to help bring others back to the subject when they have rambled or gotten off the point. In meetings and small groups it is the rule rather than the exception for one or more participants to get off the track, and lead others off track, too.

> Margene, a website manager for a soft drink manufacturer, was leading a team meeting composed of three peers in her division, two managers from sales, and one human resources representative. Sam, the company's star sales manager, was well known for his war stories about life in the sales trenches. "It's a jungle out there" was his favorite expression. The team had a strict deadline, and Margene was aware that Sam could lead the group off target. When Sam predictably began to get off on one of his tangents, Margene used the technique of asking others in the group questions to help get them back on track. She also used frequent summaries and restated the original topic.

Redirecting takes skill and a sense of balance. On the one hand, we don't want others to think we are trying to overcontrol interactions, especially in groups. We don't want to hurt our relationship with the ramblers and off-the-trackers. On the other hand, however, we can't let one or two people spoil meetings because of their self-centeredness or need for attention. Use the following suggestions to redirect others in conversations and meetings:

- Ask questions of others to get the group back on track
- Frankly explain that the topic has changed direction
- Summarize what has been said thus far
- Restate the original topic as a reminder

Blocking. Football fans understand the importance of blocking to protect the quarterback and receivers. Without blockers the defense would rush in and tackle the ball carrier with ease. When we are in conversations or meetings where people want to continue talking, but we are out of time or energy, we need to use a form of blocking as listeners.

> Marco, a paralegal for a corporate law firm, was out of time and out of energy. He was just plain tired, and he felt rushed to make his train connection. However, as he was leaving his office in downtown Atlanta on a Friday afternoon, his administrative assistant Claudia dropped by his cubicle and began talking about her weekend plans. He felt torn between trying to fake attention to Claudia and to keep moving out the door to catch the rapid transit. As a result, he gave Claudia the impression that he didn't like or value her and still missed his ride home.

Marco needed to use one or more blocking strategies to stop Claudia from continuing without alienating her. Here are a few blocking techniques that could be used:

- Stand up and push back your chair
- Look at your wristwatch
- Ask the person if you could talk more later
- Tell the person that you are running late

From the beginning we have stressed the important role both speakers and listeners play during conversations. Listening is a process that requires a feedback loop; without feedback the circle is incomplete. Learning how to give and receive feedback effectively provides a mechanism for us to improve relationships with friends, loved ones, and coworkers.

A final note. We hope you'll agree that you have the power to be successful as a listener. It is a skill that requires energy, desire to improve, and practice to master the techniques. By understanding your listening preferences and applying the ideas to your everyday relationships, you have potential to create relationships that are more satisfying, enjoyable, and fun.

REFERENCES

1. C. Hymowitz (September 7, 1999). Damark's Unique Post: A Manager Who Helps Work on Relationships. *Wall Street Journal*.
2. C. L. Dannhauser (May 1999). Shut Up and Listen. *Working Woman*, 41.
3. A. Hiam (1999). *Motivating and Rewarding Employees*. Holbrook, MA: Adams Media Corporation.
4. J. Gottman (1999). *Why Marriages Succeed or Fail . . . And How You Can Make Yours Last*. New York: Simon & Schuster. C. Lavington (1997). *You've Only Got Three Seconds*. New York: Doubleday. P. Harkins (1999). *Powerful Conversations*. New York: McGraw-Hill.

To Contact the Authors

Larry Barker: lbarker933@cs.com
Kittie Watson: kittiewatson@cs.com

For more information about listening products, tools, and materials, contact:
SPECTRA Incorporated Publishers
www.SPECTRAweb.com.

For more information about listening workshops, coaching, and consulting services, contact:
Innolect Inc.
www.innolectinc.com

To contact the International Listening Association (ILA):
IListening@aol.com

For Further Reading

Adler, M. (1997). *How to Speak, How to Listen*. New York: Collier Books.

Blanchard, K. (1999). *The Heart of a Leader*. New York: Waterbrook Press.

Bone, D. (1995). *The Business of Listening*. Los Altos, CA: Crisp Publications.

Borisoff, D. and M. Purdy (eds.) (1997). *Listening in Everyday Life: A Personal and Professional Approach*. 2nd Ed. Lanham, MD: University Press of America.

Brownell, J. (1996). *Listening: Attitudes, Principles and Skills*. Boston: Allyn and Bacon.

Burley-Allen, M. (1995). *Listening: The Forgotten Skill*. New York: John Wiley & Sons, Inc.

For Further Reading

Covey, S. (1989). *The 7 Habits of Highly Effective People*. New York: Simon & Schuster.

deLisser, P. (1999). *Be Your Own Executive Coach*. Worcester, MA: Chandler House Press.

Fromm, E. (1998). *The Art of Listening*. New York: Continuum Publishing Group.

Gottman, J. (1999). *Why Marriages Succeed or Fail . . . And How You Can Make Yours Last*. New York: Simon & Schuster.

Gray, J. (1992). *Men Are from Mars, Women Are from Venus*. New York: HarperCollins.

Gray, J. (1994). *What Your Mother Couldn't Tell You and Your Father Didn't Know*. New York: HarperCollins.

Greene, R. and J. Elffers (1998). *48 Laws of Power*. New York: Viking.

Halley, R. D. (1997). *And Then I Was Surprised by What You Said*. Columbia, MO: KAIA Publishing.

Mendell, A. (1996). *How Men Think*. New York: Fawcett Columbine.

Michaelson, S. A. (1999). *Is Anyone Listening? Repairing Broken Lives in Couples Communication*. New York: Prospect Books.

Mindell, P. (1995). *A Woman's Guide to the Language of Success*. Paramus, NJ: Prentice Hall.

Nichols, M. (1996). *The Lost Art of Listening: How Learning to Listen Can Improve Relationships*. New York: Guilford Press.

Peters, T. (1999). *Reinventing Work: The Professional Service Firm*. New York: Alfred A. Knopf, Inc.

Ryan, K. D. and D. K. Oestreich (1997 2nd Ed.). *Driving Fear Out of the Workplace*. San Francisco: Jossey-Bass Publishers.

Senge, P. M., C. Roberts, R. B. Ross, B. J. Smith, and A. Kleiner. (1994). *The Fifth Discipline Fieldbook: Strategies and Tools for Building a Learning Organization*. New York: Doubleday.

Spence, G. (1995). *How to Argue and Win Every Time*. New York: St. Martin's Press.

Steil, L. K., L. L. Barker, and K. W. Watson (1983). *Effective Listening: Key to Your Success*. New York: Random House.

Tannen, D. (1990). *You Just Don't Understand: Women and Men in Conversation*. New York: William Morrow and Company.

Tannen, D. (1994). *Talking from 9 to 5*. New York: William Morrow and Company.

Watson, K. W. and L. L. Barker (1997). *Winning by Listening Around*. New Orleans, LA: SPECTRA, Inc.

Wolvin, A. and C. G. Coakley (1996). *Listening* (5th Ed.). Madison: Brown & Benchmark.

Index

woman out on a date, went to the wrong restaurant because she listened poorly, 85

woman receives many invitations to parties because she listens, 10–12

woman self-monitors her listening energy, then deals with her mother, 70

woman who can't remain silent, 110

worker who didn't accept negative feedback well, and was fired, 176–77

worker who had the flu, and couldn't focus on listening, 71

worker who has little listening energy left over for family, 61

young employee who planned to change her listening style, but didn't actually take action, 99–100

young student so excited by her report card that she can't make sense, 181

Challenger disaster, 162

children, young
  listening to, 143–46
  role models for listening behavior of, 7–8, 144–46
  tips for talking to, 145–46

Clark, A., 142

clock watching, while listening, 28

Coakley, C. G., 141, 154

Cohen, S. S., 122

communication
  axiom that what can be misunderstood, will be, 156
  controlled by listeners, not speakers, 1–17, 180–84
  feedback in, 169–84
  keeping open channels of, for teens, 148

content-oriented listeners, 26–28
  cues to assessing, personal and office/environmental, 48
  speaking adapted to, 49
  strengths and weaknesses of, 27–28

conversations

gender differences in, 129–32
  multiple, in a crowded room, listening to, 129
  redirected to get back on track, 182

counselors, men as, 133

couples. *See* marriage; spouses

couples listening workshops, 13

Covey, S., 103

co-workers
  assessing their listening styles, 45
  giving specific feedback to, 174

CPAs, listening styles of, 35

criticism, selective, when talking to teenagers, 148

Cusella, L., 18

Damark Direct Sales Corporation, 169

dampening technique for controlling a conversation, 180–81

Dannhauser, Carol L., 184
  quote by, 170

dates, talking too much on, xviii

day people, 78–79

daydreaming, not listening due to, 93–94

Dear Abby column, quotes from, 109, 164

DeRopp, R. S., *The Master Game,* quote from, 72

dinner business meetings, conversing effectively at, xviii

directions, reading, when everything else fails, 12

distractions
  tuning out, sex differences in, 129, 135–36
  when talking to children, avoiding, 145
  yielding to, and not listening, 92–93

ditch, analogy of a troubled person in a, 151–52

Do You Love Me listening pitfall, 60–61

doing more than one thing at a time, 61–62

Donnovan, P., 141

Index

Index